A WORD IN YOUR EAR

*Dedicated, with sincere thanks, to my sister Ann Cooper,
and her husband Brian,
whose whispered words of affirmation and encouragement
were there for me when really needed.*

Jack McArdle ss cc

A Word in Your Ear

WHISPERINGS ON CHRISTIAN LIVING

the columba press

First published in 2002 by
the columba press
55A Spruce Avenue, Stillorgan Industrial Park,
Blackrock, Co Dublin

Cover by Bill Bolger
Cover photo: Marie Mc Donald
Origination by The Columba Press
Printed in Ireland by ColourBooks Ltd, Dublin

ISBN 1 85607 371 8

Contents

Introduction

I have enjoyed writings these reflections. I wrote them for myself, knowing that, if they helped me, they might also be a help to others. I chose words that came to me spontaneously, and put them in the order in which they came. I deliberately, however, selected Humility as the opening reflection, because I believe that if I can get this one right, the others will be possible. Without humility, there is no hope of being compassionate, forgiving, accepting, or grateful. Humility is the mother of all the virtues.

Through reflecting on these words, it is my hope that we might become more aware of what they involve, and be more open to practising the virtue in our daily living. While the Spirit is the principal catalyst of Christian living, it is necessary that we be open to that practice, and be willing to take that on board. On occasions throughout these reflections I turn to the Spirit with a prayer. This generally comes at a time when I become acutely aware that I am expounding on something that is the preserve of the Spirit, and that it would be a travesty if I continued without acknowledging that fact. The action of the Spirit is much more important than anything I could say.

The list included is not exhaustive. There are so many other words that could have been included, but I felt that the twenty I chose is more than enough to go on with. I chose them because they are part of our everyday experience, and any one of us can practise these virtues any day we wish. Because the word 'virtue' might seem too abstract and pious, I prefer to think of them as personality traits of the Christian. Living the Christian life is about giving witness, and displaying some or all of these traits in our behaviour is a sure and certain witness. Christianity is about attracting, rather than promoting. What I am is my message, rather than anything I say. I entrust these reflections to my readers with a great sense of privilege and gratitude. I pray that the Spirit may anoint you in the reading, as I feel he anointed me in the writing. We live in a world in need of healing, in need of good influences. As Christians, we are called to be the leaven in society. Even when we doubt the power of influence at our disposal, or when we fail to see any good effect coming from our efforts, we can continue to live in faith that our lives lived in selfless service take on a purpose and a value that will resonate throughout eternity. How truly blessed we are ...

Humility

I deliberately chose humility as the first subject for reflection, because I believe that if we can get this one right, it will have long and far-reaching benefits in our lives. I have always had a problem with humility, not as a concept, but as something I could look at objectively, and understand its ramifications. I got off to a very bad start in the humility stakes. I grew up with a 'children should be seen and not heard' philosophy, and praise was very scarce on the ground. I remember getting a good school report one time (the only time?), and when my mother looked at it, she put it away without comment. I was yearning for a word of praise or approval, but it was believed that praise was dangerous, because it caused one's head to expand! When my aunt visited, I actually hid behind the bedroom door, 'earwigging' to hear if my mother would mention my school report to her!

Humility, in fact, is something very simple. It is better understood when it is called Truth. It comes from a realisation and acceptance of the truth as it is. 'Realisation' and 'reality' are first cousins. It is about learning to live with reality, and not in some make-believe world. Some people find it difficult to live it reality, because it can be quite painful. I have an alcoholic friend who, after several years of sobriety, went back drinking because he couldn't live with the realities of his life.

For the purpose of this reflection, and those following, I have no desire to expound in psychological jargon or to wear my behavioural scientist's hat. If humility is of such central importance, I want to try to present it in a realistic and understandable way, so that we might be more inclined to practise it. I want to go directly to Jesus, to look at him, to watch him, to learn from him. 'Learn from me, because I am meek and humble of heart.' We are told that Jesus did not cling to his equality with God, but humbled himself even to death on the cross. That was why God raised him above all, gave him a name above all names, so that, at his name, every knee should bow. Mary, who was his first teacher, tells us that God raises up the lowly, and knocks the proud from their thrones. No matter what I say about humility, I am totally convinced that it is only the Spirit of God who can lead us to an understanding, appreciation, and practice of this wonderful virtue

Before going any further, I suggest a prayer right now: *Spirit and breath of God, please lead me into truth, as Jesus promised. Let me see myself, and the circumstances of my life, as they really are. Please do not allow me to wander in an unreal world of fantasy, vainglory, and deceit. Please free me from all self-delusion, and from all need to portray myself as something that I am not.*

Jesus was a down-to-earth God. He could have loved us from a distance, but he chose to come among us, and to meet us where we're at. That included sitting at table with sinners, touching the leper, and speaking to the prostitute. It was this quality in him that endeared him to these people. They were not used to that from their religious leaders and teachers. No wonder they followed him everywhere he went, because his message is about attracting rather than promoting. Love is to accept another exactly as that person is, and to be willing to help that person move on, if he or she wishes to. Humility is love in practice. *Humilitas* is the Latin for 'of the ground', which comes from *humus*, the Latin for 'clay'. Of ourselves we are subject to the law of gravity and, by ourselves, we cannot rise out of the quicksand of our own selfishness. Jesus became exactly like us – he was tempted as we are, and he chose not to avail of his own divine powers in his struggles. Rather, before his public mission, he opened his heart to the power of the Spirit when he went down into the Jordan river in baptism. He then proceeded to live and to act in the power of that Spirit, and to clearly demonstrate to us that, with the Spirit, we can live as he did. Once again, we speak of the Spirit of truth, which is another way of saying the Spirit of Humility.

Original sin was a lie that was brought about by Satan, the father of lies. The antidote, the antibiotic for that is the truth. That is what Jesus means when he says that the truth will set us free. Jesus continually challenged the Pharisees and the other religious leaders about their parade of virtue, and how they were living a lie. He lays such a store on humility that their behaviour and their attitude revolted him. They represented the exact opposite to the values and principles he proclaimed. Original sin was a lie, it was disobedience, it was a declaration that we would do things our way, because that was superior to the way set out by God. It was a complete rejection of our place before God. It was usurping the divine role, and it was surely anathema in the eyes of God.

It is important to know our place before God. He is the potter, we are the clay, the work of his hands. All the pain that is being inflicted on the church at the moment will renew it as with a new Pentecost, when we will have a humbler church, less strident in its righteousness, and more in touch with the reality of people's suffering, and its mission to speak to such people of love, of hope, and of forgiveness. To paraphrase part of a poem from Patrick Kavanagh, 'When a man finds himself lying on the ground, face downwards, with his nose buried in the rubble of his achievements, he is ready to be wafted across the chasm of infested waters into a land of hope, of new birth, and of new beginnings.' When the church has imbibed a good strong dose of humility, it will be renewed in an exciting and extraordinary way.

Cardinal Mercier wrote: 'I am going to reveal to you a secret of sanctity and happiness. If every day, for five minutes, you keep your imagination quiet, shut your eyes to all the things of sense, and close your ears to all the sounds of earth, so as to be able to withdraw into the sanctuary of your baptised soul, which is the temple of the Holy Spirit, speaking there to that Holy Spirit thus:

O Holy Spirit, I adore you. Enlighten, guide, strengthen, and console me. Tell me what I ought to do, and command me to do it. I promise to be submissive in everything that you permit to happen to me; only show me what is your will.'

'If you love me, you will obey me", says Jesus. Obeying him is my way of declaring that I belong to him. People in twelve-step programmes, recovering from an addiction, are given these two prayers to say as part of that journey:

God, I offer myself to you, to build with me, and to do with me as you will. Relieve me of the bondage to self, that I may better do your will.

And again:

My Creator, I am now willing that you should have all of me, good and bad. I pray that you should remove from me every single defect of character that stands in the way of my usefulness to you, and to others. Give me strength, as I go out from here, to do your bidding.

Accepting reality in my life is humility. I could write down the facts as they are. Humility is to accept those facts: I am mortal; I will die. Everything I do by myself is also mortal, and will also die. The first time I was carried into a church (Baptism) I was not consulted; the next time I'll be carried into a church (funeral), I won't be consulted either! To try to run the show in the meantime is insanity. I can change my outer appearance. I can lose weight, grow a beard, or change my clothes. I cannot, however, change *myself* in any way. It is only the Creator who can recreate me. I am absolutely powerless over the demons within, and it is only God who can cleanse the temple of my heart.

St Paul cried out: 'Who will free me from the slavery to this deadly human nature? Thank God, it has been done through Jesus Christ our Lord.' The first thing I have to do is to stop playing God. God becomes God in my life the moment I surrender, and let him take over. Humility is about things being the way they ought to be.

I referred earlier to the false notions of humility I might easily have inherited in earlier life. Spirituality tended to emphasise the evil condition of human nature, and there was a real possibility of accepting that I was worthless, no better than a worm in the ground. Nothing could be farther from the truth, and such thinking has nothing whatever to do with humility, because it is not true. I am good, because God created me and, to quote Herb Barks, 'God don't make no junk.' What is true, however, is that everything I have is gift, and that I myself own nothing. One heart attack, and my life is ended. If I can speak, see, hear, walk, or write, it is because God chose to give me those gifts. There are people who did not get one or more of those gifts. Any gifts God gave me are given for the sake of others, and I certainly cannot claim any personal credit for them. God didn't give me my gift of speech to go around talking to myself! A proper appreciation of the gifts I have should fill my heart with constant gratitude. 'He that is mighty has done great things for me, and holy is his name.'

The more I magnify the Lord the more obvious will my littleness be. Mary was absolutely humble and, therefore, she was filled with awe at how generous God had been to her. She gave all the credit to God, while acknowledging that she was truly blessed indeed. In a way, I will be continuing this theme of humility in the following chapter, when I go on to reflect on gratitude. To be filled with gratitude for the gift of life, and all the gifts that go to make up that life, is one sure way 'to walk humbly with your God.'

Gratitude

It is not possible to be grateful and unhappy at the same time. Gratitude is a beautiful virtue, and it was something much appreciated by Jesus. How often does he begin a prayer with 'I thank you, Father, Lord of heaven and earth ...' Before he multiplied the loaves and fish, before he called Lazarus from the tomb, or before he broke the bread at the Last Supper, he spoke a word of thanks to the Father. When he healed the ten lepers, he was hurt and disappointed that only one of them returned to give thanks. Jesus would often have used the psalms as his prayers, and many of them are songs of praise and thanks.

'How sharper than a serpent's tooth it is to have a thankless child,' are the words that Shakespeare puts in the mouth of King Lear. To be grateful is an expression of humility, as referred to in the previous chapter. This expression of humility causes one to have a constant sense of awe at the goodness of God, and the goodness of others. A proud person could never experience gratitude, because everything that is done for them is seen as something that is theirs by right. I have often noticed a banquet scene in a movie where the waiters carry trays of food, pour out glasses of wine, remove all empty plates, and they go completely unnoticed by those they serve. It is almost as if it were a sign of weakness to thank a waiter. Indeed, I have often seen something similar in real life. Why should I thank the barber, the mechanic, or the garbage man, when I am paying for the service they provide? I might even believe that they owe me a debt of gratitude for giving them the work in the first place.

In my dealing with the elderly, there is something I have noticed with some of them. No matter how confused, forgetful, or mixed up some of them might be, they express gratitude for every single thing that is done for them. It is almost as if it were automatic, where the habit of a lifetime continues, amidst all the confusion and loss of awareness. I have come across individuals who were unique in this area, and it never ceased to impress me. I didn't know many of them during their earlier years, but I can easily imagine what they were like. Under normal circumstances, we can take it for granted that this is something instilled in the child from early on. 'What do you say?' 'Oh, sorry, thanks.' 'That's better.' This is good, of course, but we should not underestimate the positive effect of constant good example in this area for the child. Children tend to mimic, and to imitate, and parents do well to lead the way in their example of expressing gratitude and appreciation.

Gratitude to God is directly linked to humility. The more aware I am of the vast gap between creature and Creator, the more in awe I am at God's goodness to me. When I am convinced that it is pure gift, and it has not been earned, nor is it deserved, the more grateful I am. When I am aware of being under the Niagara of the Father's love, my heart is filled with songs and prayers of thanks. This thanks need not be expressed in words, but in a song I hum, a sense of well-being I experience, or a smile on my face, even when I am alone. (If you're happy, tell your face, and then we'll all know!) When I speak of knowing my place before God, I am speaking of the contrast between God and myself, of a vast gap that exists between the extremes of that relationship. It is impossible for my human mind to grasp the fullness of the concept of God's love. To come into this awareness is uniquely the work of the Spirit. Let us turn to the Spirit now:

Spirit and breath of God, please reveal the Father's love to me.
Please enlighten my mind, my heart, and my soul with a deep

conviction of this love. May it be embedded in my heart, and may it directly effect my approach to God and my on-going relationship with him. Please continue to remind me of his love. 'Seek you first the kingdom of God … and everything else will be added …' I don't think it is an exaggeration to say that if I concentrated on seeking the kingdom of God, and of living by the rules of that kingdom, I wouldn't have to ask God for anything, because 'everything else would be added …' In other words, my only prayer would be one of thanksgiving. My grateful attitude, and my prayers of thanks and praise are a direct foreshadowing of my eternity in heaven. The road to heaven is heaven, and it would be a wonderful grace to begin my praise and thanksgiving now. Although my thanks is prompted by my own sense of well-being, it is concentrated more on God than on myself. God is the object of my prayer. In prayers of petition, I myself can be the object. I can be quite selfish in my prayer, when I myself am at the centre of my concern. Prayers of thanksgiving shift the focus onto God. My thanks should not be confined to what God has given me, or done for me. I can thank him for the goodness of his nature, for the vastness of his love, for the immensity of his generosity. I will find many beautiful prayers of thanksgiving among the psalms, prayers that were very familiar to Jesus. In our ordinary day-to-day conversation, there are frequent references to thanking God. 'It's a lovely day, thank God … I'm keeping well, thanks be to God … Thank God for small mercies.' One old Irish lady is credited with the comment, 'We should never be off our knees thanking God that we're able to stand up.'

Let me return to Mary again, for a moment. She was the one person who had a perfect relationship with God. She was deeply aware of her place before God. Her *Magnificat* is a truly wonderful prayer, and a very practical example for us in the art of prayer. Her heart is brimming over with thanks and praise. After the Annunciation, she was faced with a quandary. Who could she tell? Who would understand her? There was only one person, and that was Elizabeth, who herself had some kind of similar experience. When they met, they broke forth in praise and thanks to God, because he had done such great things for both of them. Sentence after sentence of the *Magnificat* is a litany of all the blessings of the Lord. He is so wonderful, so extraordinarily generous, so deeply aware of her lowly state, and so faithful with all his promises. This God of hers was totally reliable, and she had no hesitation whatever in saying her 'Yes' to whatever he asked of her. He was a God of great love, of fidelity, of compassion, and of tender mercy. No wonder she would tell the servants at Cana to do exactly what Jesus told them, because she trusted his goodness completely. It is easy to imagine that her prayer was one of constant thanks and praise.

In writing these reflections, it is my hope and prayer to highlight important topics so that they might be integrated into our lives. It is hoped that we can gain new insights, and that we might be motivated to act on some of them. I believe it is important to develop a grateful heart towards God, and towards others. It is a beautiful quality to have, and everybody, including myself, gains immensely from it. I said at the beginning of this reflection that it is not possible to be grateful and unhappy at the same time. To develop a sense of gratitude, and to give expression to that gratitude, is a sure way of bringing one out of oneself. We can so easily become tied up in ourselves, and in everything that concerns us, to the exclusion of everyone else around us. I can end up in my own self-inflicted solitary confinement, when the only person in my life is myself. I can lose all sense of gratitude, either because I believe that everybody else owes me something, or I am so preoccupied with myself that I haven't time to think of others. Developing a sense of gratitude can relieve me from the prison of self. It can free me from the bondage of self-pity, resentment, and self-preoccupation. There is so much to be gained from developing a grateful heart. It is my hope, in these reflections, not just to add to the discussion, but to inspire some decision. I am hoping that these reflections might be received as calls to action.

To follow through on my train of thought would bring me, naturally, to reflect on affirmation, confirmation, and acknowledgment of the good in others. This is a practical way in which my gratitude can be expressed.

Affirmation

Affirmation and confirmation are interchangeable, as words, as I will use them. They speak of the act of acknowledging the worth of another person, or approving the work of that person. It is the opposite to knocking or pulling down another, something with which we are all familiar. It is about building up, about encouraging others in themselves, and in their work. It makes others feel good about themselves, and this is something that we all need, and we all seek. It is not flattery or false praise, because it is real affirmation only if it's the truth. Just as we can have false concepts of humility, so we can easily misunderstand affirmation. Humility is truth, and affirmation is speaking the truth about another, when that truth is helpful, and needs to be said.

The real issue here, of course, is how I feel about myself. I cannot give what I haven't got. The day I feel good about me, I think you're OK too. And the day I don't feel good about me, then God help those around me! It is as if there was a slide projector in my head, that projects pictures onto others, and to situations and circumstances of my life. If the picture is negative, what I see will be negative. A man pulled up at a filling-station one day, and he asked the pump attendant, 'What are the people like in this next village down there?' The attendant replied, 'What were they like in that last village you came through?' 'Oh, they were very nice, and friendly.' 'Ah, well, you'll find the people in the next village will be nice and friendly also.' Another man turned up, and asked the same question.

When the pump attendant asked him what the people in the last village were like, he was told they were sour, dour, and unfriendly. 'Ah, well,' said the attendant, 'you'll find the people in the next village will be exactly like that.' If I listen into a conversation where two people are criticising a third person, the conversation can tell me more about the two who are talking than about the person being discussed.

The gospels give us some wonderful examples of the relationship between the three Persons of the Trinity. Jesus is continually extolling the Father. The Father speaks from the clouds to announce how pleased he is with Jesus. Jesus speaks glowingly of the Spirit, and all he will do when he comes. He also says that the Spirit will tell us all about him, and the Spirit will confirm his message. The love within the Trinity is expressed through affirmation, through affirming the role and importance of the other. There is no upstaging here, because that would be to break the unity of love, and to contradict their common purpose. They were of one mind and heart in bringing our salvation to completion. Their love is best expressed in their unity, and it is openly expressed in their affirmation and acknowledgement of each other. For a group of Christians, for example, to claim to be sharing in the life of the Trinity, it would be essential that we could clearly identify their constant affirmation of each other. Each would reflect the glory and goodness of God to the other.

A sure sign that I have the Spirit of God within is my willingness to confirm others. Confirmation has always been associated with giving the Spirit. The Spirit of God within will always show itself in this way, and my ability and willingness to confirm others is the surest sign there is that I have had a Pentecost. St Paul speaks about learning to live and to walk in the Spirit. Those who live in the Spirit are easily recognised because they are noted for confirming others. It is part of the work of the Spirit to give confirmation, but a Spirit without a body cannot do any-thing. An evil spirit needs somebody's hands to plant the bomb, or somebody's tongue to tell the lie. Similarly, the Holy Spirit needs our voices to confirm others. The Spirit needs us as channels of this confirmation. When we live and walk in the Spirit, we confirm others without even being conscious of it. It just becomes a way of life for us. We would not at all be into the business of knocking others, or putting others down. I suggest we might say the follow-ing prayer:

Spirit and breath of God, I offer myself to you, to use me as you see fit. Please speak through me, continue your work through me. Inspire my words and actions so that they may contribute to the building of the kingdom. I make myself available to do your work.

Knocking others, or putting them down is not part of the work of the Spirit. I can trust that the Spirit will accept my offer, and will use me in the building of the kingdom of God.

There is an enormous explosion of workshops, pro-grammes, literature, and courses on the whole area of building up one's self-image. Many people are severely damaged because of a bad self-image, a lack of confidence, or the absence of any feeling of self-worth. Years of put-down can result in long-term destruction of a person's feeling of well-being. I myself believe that constant affirm-ation from a good friend can be more effective in repairing this damage than all the workshops one could attend. The workshops, by their nature, tend to be removed from our everyday reality. The most effective help is given in the or-dinary everyday situations, provided, of course, that it is constant and ongoing. To build up another's sense of self-worth is a very practical way of loving. Mother Teresa used to say that the greatest hunger in today's world is not for food, but for love. All those starving millions we see on our television screens certainly need food, but they also need a sense of dignity, and of self-worth. They have no reason to believe that they are more than just pawns in a deadly game of greed and selfish violence. They need a voice and a hand that will reach out to them, and restore some of the dignity and sense of worth that has been so cruelly wrenched from them.

Jesus was expert at raising people up, and giving them dignity. He is the greatest example we have of what it means to confirm others. He was to be found with the outcasts of society, with those who had nothing left to lose. He was accused of welcoming sinners, and even eating with them. He probably smiled when he heard this accusation, because it showed that, for once, his accusers were speaking the truth. To understand how he acted towards the outcasts and down-and-outs, it is necessary to understand the mind-set among the Jews of that time. There were many untouchables, and there were even more that were beyond the pale of recognition as human beings. A prostitute was about to be stoned to death, because this was what she was considered to deserve. What did Jesus do? He defended her, spoke to her, obtained her freedom, and gave her a word of advice. On another occasion, when he was in the house of one of the Pharisees, a woman recognised by all as a public sinner came in, approached him, fell at his feet, began to wash his feet with her tears, and wipe them with her hair. This was a tense moment, as all eyes were on him to see what he would do. He shocked them all by declaring that she had done more for him than the Pharisee who was entertaining him. He spoke of her great love, and he said that what she had done would forever and always be remembered. That woman took an extraordinary risk, but her trust in Jesus was well founded. Whatever the reason, she just seemed to know what kind of person he was, and she was not disappointed. Extraordinary affirmation indeed. Lepers were certainly outside the pale for the Jews, and yet we have Jesus touching a leper, and speaking kindly to others. He spoke to the Samaritan woman, who had two strokes against her – she was a woman, and she was a Samaritan. 'If you love those who love you, what reward can you expect? Even the pagans do that, do they not?' said Jesus. To extend this to the lowest in society, and to those who were outside the accepted norm for common courtesy, was something extraordinary indeed. We are asked to follow Jesus, which means to follow his example, and not just to admire him. This is a serious challenge to all of us who claim to be Christian, and to bear his name.

The following short verse speaks to us of how we should treat others while they are alive, and not wait 'till they're dead before speaking well of them.

> I would rather have a little rose
> From the garden of a friend,
> Than to have the choicest flowers
> When my stay on earth must end.
> I would rather have the little words,
> And a smile that I can see,
> Than flattery when my heart is still,
> And life has ceased to be.
> I would rather have a loving smile
> From friends I know are true,
> Than tears shed round my casket
> When this world I bid adieu.
> I want the flowers while I am here,
> Be they pink or white or red.
> I'd rather have one blossom now
> Than a truckload when I'm dead.

Honesty

As I write this, I am thinking that, if I had the ability, I would love to write a whole book on Humility, and another one on Honesty. They are extremely attractive virtues, and to have them is a wonderful foundation for a fruitful Christian life. Honesty has always appealed to me, even when I was conscious of being less than honest in my words or actions. My dictionary defines honesty as 'fair and upright in speech and act; not lying, cheating, or stealing; sincere.' All of these would be very wonderful traits of character for a full and wholesome life.

At the time of writing there is much talk about transparency in government, in church, and in business generally. In recent times we have had more than enough of dishonesty and cover-up in high places. We speak of someone 'being economical with the truth', which is just another way of saying that the person is telling lies. While we would all welcome more of the transparency we hear about, I have a problem with much of what surrounds the concept in public life today. When the communication highways continue to explode at an enormous rate, we find that more and more information is available about institutions and individuals. It is becoming more and more difficult to cover-up any more, as the spotlight of the media focuses in on the back-pockets of politicians, the vaults of banks, and the files of institutions, including the church. My problem is that honesty might become expedient, it might become something that is forced on people who would willingly go the other direction if the climate was right.

Honesty is a way of thinking, a way of living, a way of being. It is not something that I can pick up and lay aside as I please. For honesty to have any credibility, there must be a consistency about it. It involves a fundamental option in my life, a direction in which I wish my life to go. It involves integrity, sincerity, and genuineness. It is such a major quality of character that it deeply effects every aspect of my life. It is the pearl of great price that is spoken of in the gospel, which, when it is found, one should give up everything that gets in the way to get it. It is difficult to distinguish between honesty and truth. I would suggest that honesty is truth in action. It is something that grows within the human heart, before it translates into words and actions.

Honesty is essentially the work of the Spirit. Satan is called the father of lies, and honesty is the evidence of freedom from bondage. To live with honesty is to live with God's Spirit.

Spirit and breath of God, I ask you, please, to instill in my heart the gift of honesty. Rid my heart of all duplicity, double-dealing, or false compromises. Please lead me in the way of integrity and uprightness. Sow the seeds of honesty in the soil of my soul that it may produce fruits that are worthy of the kingdom.

I switch over to a prayer from time to time because, no matter what words I use, or how I attempt to explain a concept, it is the Holy Spirit alone who can instill that virtue. Only God can do a God-thing. The Spirit has come to complete the work of salvation in our lives. Honesty is one of the fruits of the Spirit. The gifts of wisdom, discernment, and knowledge enable me to grasp the centrality of a virtue like honesty, and it is uniquely the gift of the Spirit that prompts me to develop and practise that virtue.

It is no exaggeration to say that Jesus' honesty got him into trouble on many occasions, and contributed to his death eventually. He was never prepared to compromise his truth. He was completely authentic in everything he did and said. This was obvious even to the little children, who are particularly sharp at discovering someone who is genuine. One person can pick up a child and play with her, while, if someone else tries it they will be met with cries and tears. The children recognised this special quality in Jesus, and so he was able to hug them.

We are told that the essence of proper communication is to be able to combine total honesty with total kindness. I could visit someone in hospital today, and when he asks me how I think he looks, I tell him that he looks awful, and will probably die this evening. I am being totally honest, while being brutally unkind. On the other hand, just to curry favour, I could turn a blind eye to some young people using drugs, or engaged in vandalism. I am being kind, but very dishonest, because I totally disapprove of what they are doing. Jesus told the woman, 'Neither do I condemn you. Go your way, and sin no more.' He did not condemn her, and yet he did not say that what she did was OK. Jesus came with a mission. That mission was clearly defined by the Father. Its terms did not change, nor did the emphasis vary. He was single-minded in that mission, and he was consistent in his fidelity to that mission.

Honesty flows from that single-minded approach to life. Why am I on this earth? Am I here to manipulate others, to get all I can at the expense of others, to wriggle my way through life without reference to others? If I hold myself responsible for how I relate to others, then that will totally depend on how honest I can be. Honesty in relationships is not something that is held in high regard today. With the break-down in the moral fibre of society, there seems to be less emphasis on the importance of fidelity in marriage, and of loyalty in the work-place. We see this also in big business where, when the local work-force have given of their best to establish the business, the powers-that-be up-root the business to go elsewhere where labour is cheaper.

Honesty includes loyalty, and loyalty is something to be treasured.

We get little glimpses in the gospel where Jesus is seen to be annoyed. On several occasions he asked the Pharisees questions, and when they refused to answer, because their answer would trip themselves up, he is seen to be disgusted with them. 'What did your fathers do? ... Whose head and superscription is this? ... Which do you think is easier to say: "Your sins are forgiven", or "arise and walk"?' On such occasions he is seen to just leave them there. If that is what they wanted, that is what they would get. Herod asked him 'What is truth?', and he walked away without waiting for the answer. Jesus was quick to detect the deceits of Satan, whether that was in the desert, in the possessed, or when Peter tried to persuade him not to go up to Jerusalem. 'My strength is as the strength of ten, because my heart is pure.' Because he had an honest disposition, he could detect deceit and cunning immediately. The search-light of his look showed up all the shades and shadows. I have often imagined that if I were in the presence of Jesus back those times, I would be very conscious of the fact that he could read my innermost being, and I would be particularly careful to be honest. I remember asking the priest who took care of Padre Pio in the latter years of his life, what it felt like to be with someone who could see you through and through. He smiled and replied, 'It helped me to be very good!' I can imagine how Jesus must have rejoiced to look within the heart of his mother. She was 100% genuine, 100% authentic. In the old days, a sculptor in Rome, while chipping away at the marble, putting the final touches to a statue, might accidentally chip off something that should have been left. Instead of dumping the statue, he would use some wax, mixed with marble dust, and fill up the small hole and, after the wax had hardened, that spot would not be noticed by us mere amateurs. A statue that was 100% marble, without flaw, was marked *sine cera,* which literarily means *without wax.* It is from this that we get the word 'sincere', which implies something that is 100% genuine.

The liar has to have a good memory. It can often take many lies to cover up the first one. The honest person can have a peaceful sleep. It becomes awkward when I have to rack my memory to know what was the last story I told. This can make for a very furtive and edgy lifestyle. There is a wonderful freedom in truth. 'The truth shall set you free,' says Jesus. The facts are friendly and, when everything else fails, it's worth trying the truth. The truth always works.

There is a certain amount of cynicism today about the absence of honesty in business and in politics. Some would go so far as to say that it's impossible to get to the top in politics without doing several deals with the devil, in the shape of kick-backs and favours. We are all familiar with workmen bringing home items from the workplace for home use, or a builder or tradesman cutting corners on a job. It is difficult to trust people any more. Unfortunately, we will always have this, but there is something I can do about it. If I'm not part of the solution, I remain as part of the problem. By my own personal honesty I am contributing something significant to the overall picture. The fact that others are dishonest is never an excuse for me to do the same. 'Sure, everyone does it,' is an excuse we sometimes hear. I have to live my life according to my own moral standards, and I will be judged on my own decisions and acts, and not on the behaviour of others. My honesty can be all the more worthy if it is lived out in the midst of intrigue and subterfuge. Honesty always wins out in the final analysis and, as a Christian, I have no choice. What I speak about here is Christian living. The real value of Christian living is its witness value. 'You shall be my witnesses onto the ends of the earth ...'

Hope

The only real sin I can commit, as a Christian, is not to have hope. We are a resurrected people, who enjoy the victory even over death itself. It is vital that I align myself so close to Jesus that I see myself inheriting everything that he earned for me through his life, death, and resurrection. When he took on our human nature, he took on my human nature and, therefore, I stand directly to benefit personally from everything he achieved. I live with the 'sure and certain hope' that is spoken of in the letter to the Hebrews. When I speak of hope, I am not speaking of being optimistic, which can be a natural characteristic. I am speaking of a hope that is the direct result of my alignment with Jesus as my Saviour, Lord, and God. 'There is nothing impossible for God.' This is the hope that can survive trials, tribulations and failures. It is a gift, and unless I neglect it, or reject it, God will not take it away.

There is tremendous need for hope in today's world. Many people live in dark depression, and can see no way out. There is an alarming rise in suicides, especially among the young. The church is going through a time of trial at the moment, and many good people are beginning to lose hope that it can survive. It is particularly sad to witness this because, for a Christian, to lose hope is a contradiction in terms. I will speak about the church later on. Suffice it to say for now that, as a Christian, I believe that Jesus has the victory and, even if evil is seen to have passing success, that good will finally triumph.

Because I want to clarify that last sentence, I will speak of the church now. I believe that God saw the church as

29

badly in need of renewal. Thousands of years of human involvement can bring a watering-down, a corruption, and a
shift of focus of the message given to us to proclaim. John
the Baptist is a figure who points to the role of the church.
He gave his message, pointed to Jesus, and told the people
to follow him. He was not the Messiah, and he was very
definite in asserting this. He was but a sign-post, pointing
out to people where salvation was to be found. In my day,
I saw the church pointing to itself as the source of salvation, and we were told that outside the church there was
no salvation. When good people, prompted by the Spirit of
God, began to look elsewhere for salvation, it created
shock among the ranks of the official church. It is almost as
if we were shocked that people should leave the church to
follow Jesus! I depend totally on the Spirit here, to help us
discern what has really happened, and where the truth
lies.

> *Spirit and breath of God, please enlighten my mind to the
> truth that I need to see as I reflect on where the church is at
> now. Please show me what you believe I should know in order
> to dissipate any confusion and wrong thinking. Please give
> me the eyes of a loving prophet, as I look at the church today,
> so that I can discern the truth and the reality, free of all con-
> fusion, fault-finding, and despair.*

There are certain things that are not negotiable, certain
things that are fixed and sure. God is in charge, and Jesus
has made clear and definite promises. In this lies my hope.
I have to be humble enough to accept that, because the
church is made up of people like me, it will always be in
need of purification and renewal. There are three things:
Jesus, the gospel, and the church. Jesus is the same yesterday, today, and forever. Not one word of the gospel has
changed. The church, made up of us sinful mortals, is always in need of being brought back on target, and of being
reminded of the vision of that original mission entrusted
to it. I began to speak about the church earlier than I had

intended in this reflection, because of something I said at the end of the second last paragraph. I implied that the church would triumph over all evil, which is true, but I may have given the impression that every trial through which the church is going at the moment was the work of some evil force. I do not believe that. I am totally convinced that all of this is necessary, and all of this is for the good, and that the church is being purified and renewed in the fires of tribulation. What's at stake here is the truth, and all cover-up, all self-righteousness, and all forms of religious pride is being exposed and exorcised. This is a process that will bring the church back on track again, a much humbler and holier church. I honestly believe that this is a wonderful time for the church, and it is here precisely that the hope I speak of is needed. The test of a person's maturity is his/her ability to survive in a state of ambiguity. This is the difficult part. I can safely take it that this process of renewal will not be complete in my lifetime. The hope of which I speak, however, enables me to believe that that renewal will happen, and a newly resurrected church will once again be seen to be faithful to its mission. In the way of things, we can be sure that we will be back where we are now many years from now, just as we have been here on many occasions in the past.

Hope, on a personal level, is essential for healthy and wholesome living. 'Always have an explanation ready to give to those who ask you the reason for the hope that you have', advises Peter. If I am a Christian, I live by the promises of Jesus. My generation grew up on promises. I was making promises on New Year's Day, Ash Wednesday, at annual Retreats, and whenever a plane hit turbulence in the sky! If I was really aware of what was happening, of course, I would have noticed that I was always making the same promises. Not very successful! One of the advantages of the years is that, hopefully, we become more conscious of our human limitations, and our inability to manage life in any sort of on-going way. There comes a moment of grace, hopefully, when it dawns on me that maybe I'm coming at this the wrong way round. Instead of making promises to the Lord, I begin to listen to his promises, and to reflect on them. 'Heaven and earth will pass away before my promises pass away.' Elizabeth said to Mary, 'All these things happened to you because you believed that the promises of the Lord would be fulfilled.' The outcome of this is that I stop making promises to God, and I begin to accept and to act on his promises. In this lies my hope. Relying on fidelity to my own promises is a sure and certain entrance into the path of failure and despair. The secret of real hope is that it is not invested in myself. My hope is founded completely on the promises of Jesus, and what he has made possible for me. This gives eternal hope for life, and for hereafter.

Part of the work of a Christian is to give hope to others. My vocation is not to work to get to heaven. I will get to heaven, because Jesus died to get me to heaven, and I believe that. 'Our salvation is the result of his blood, and our faith …' My vocation is to contribute to getting heaven down here. There are people around me living in hell. 'Where there is despair, let me bring hope …' I cannot give what I haven't got. On the other hand, if I have hope, that will be transmitted to others without any great effort on my part. If I go into your house and tell you I have measles, when I actually have chicken-pox, which are you liable to contract?

There is tremendous need in today's world for people of hope, something that could be compared to lights shining in darkness. Without Christian hope, there is ample reason for despair on every side. There is so much deep-rooted injustice, and so many innocent victims of violence that it is easily impossible to see any light at the end of the tunnel. To even suggest that hope could possibly shine amidst such despair is to be someone who has learned the

great lesson of Easter morn, and whose hope and opti-
mism is based on that alone. Calvary wasn't exactly a
hope-filled scene. There were many of Jesus' friends who
went away from there in despair, despite the fact that he
did say he would rise again from the dead. Hope implies
some sort of stubborn faith that refuses to be extinguished,
no matter what the circumstances. Many a saintly soul has
been plunged in the dark night of the soul, where stubborn
faith was all that sustained them. Against all the odds,
they believed, and they hung in there, believing that 'this
too shall pass'. We are all familiar with a quote attributed
to Julian of Norwich: 'All will be well, and all manner of
things will be well.' That could well be a mantra for mem-
bers of the church today.

In the final analysis, hope is a gift of the Spirit. It is not
something I can conjure up and, with gritted teeth, flexed
muscles, or clenched fist, that I can force myself into.
When I accept that it is pure free gift, then I will skip the
discussion and the debate, go on my knees, and humbly
ask:

*Spirit and breath of God, I humbly ask you, please, to remove
from me every vestige of despair, and to fill my heart with
hope. Implant in my heart a deep trust in the promises of
Jesus, and help me to live with them in mind. Protect me from
the evil of despair, and lead me along the way of hope, with a
heart that is always conscious of the fact that I am walking in
the path of a risen, victorious, and all-powerful Saviour.
Continue to remind me that, because of Jesus, the victory is
already mine, and he is leading me back into the eternal celebration of that victory.*

Listening

'Learn to listen, and then listen to learn' is a very good motto. It may surprise some people to hear that we have to learn to listen. There are some people who seem to be good listeners by nature, and they are the fortunate ones. Listening can be a very positive way of helping another, because, so often, all the other person needs is a listening ear. Under normal circumstances, the other person knows whether the listening is genuine, and coming from a real interest and a desire to know, or simply a listening poise while the listener's mind is elsewhere. Creative listening generates creative sharing. My whole disposition towards the speaker can enable that person open up and perhaps unburden something that is really oppressing. A good listener can free another person, because a burden shared is often halved. A listening ear is one of the greatest gifts I can give another person. It requires time and attention, and it is always motivated by love.

We have often heard it said that we have two ears and only one mouth, so we should listen twice as much as we speak. The advice is sometimes given to take the cotton wool out of our ears and put it in our mouth instead. Quite often the thing a person needs more than anything else is a listening ear. It is much more than just a physical thing. It implies the presence of another who is a carer, and who is genuinely interested in how I am doing, and what I have to say. It is a very real way of loving, and it is an excellent form of service to others. Some people have to be listeners by nature of their work, as in psychiatry, counselling, mediation, etc. This is a vital skill in such ministry, because it enables one get an overall picture, and to form some opinion as to what is going on. This listening has much more to do than just listening to words. It involves picking up on the body language and all the other non-verbals that the other person is displaying. It involves an alertness and an attention that is concentrated and single-minded. Only then can the counsellor have any hope of being able to play back the tape of what is heard, and to seek clarification on issues that were just touched on. Words are often the weakest form of communication. When I stand with someone at a graveside, it is often more meaningful to put an arm around a shoulder, or to hold a hand, than to attempt to say anything. At times, words can get in the way of communication.

Communication is two-way, or not at all. When I am listening, I am communicating. I am communicating an interest, a concern, and a genuine love for the other. I remember a colleague of mine one time speaking of a prayer group he was trying to get off the ground. 'The problem is that half of them sit there all night and say nothing, and the other half speak all night, and say nothing!' I can speak louder with my silence than with my words. The Spirit of God works away silently within my heart. His promptings are in whispers, and prayer happens when I hear the whispers. Prayer is not so much me talking to God, who doesn't hear, as God talking to me who won't listen.

Spirit and breath of God, please help me have a listening heart. Help me spend those silent moments, so that I can hear your voice, and heed your promptings. Please continue to speak to my heart, and help me to be alert to your voice. Open the ears of my heart that I may hear your word, and heed your voice.

I always think of Mary as having a listening heart. When she heard the word 'she kept that word, and pondered it in her heart.' One of the Words spoken to her became flesh in her, and gave us our Saviour. Her attitude was based on a willingness to listen that came from having a humble spirit. She listened for each instruction, whether it was about God's plan of salvation, or where she might go from there. Her visit to Elizabeth, or the journey to Egypt and back, were not haphazard decisions. They were her response to direct promptings of the Spirit. As she pondered the word in her heart, her listening became prayer. 'Speak, Lord, your servant is listening' was her prayer, which was far removed from the trap some of us can fall into: 'Listen, Lord, your servant is speaking'!

Jesus said that he never did anything unless the Father told him. This certainly implies many hours of listening, and it gives us some understanding of those nights when he slipped away from the apostles to be alone. It was after such a night that he spoke his Sermon on the Mount, and that he chose his apostles. It is easy to imagine that Jesus had a wonderful gift for listening. His presence in the tabernacle epitomises that. It is more than just symbolic that, one after another, people come in to speak of their worries, their fears, their troubles, or their joys. His meeting with the Samaritan woman at the well is a wonderful example of how creative listening can generate creative sharing. She came at midday, when very few people would be about, because she probably didn't want to meet anybody. The fact that Jesus spoke to her at all was most unusual, because Jews did not speak to Samaritans. Under normal circumstances, she might have said something, and then withdrawn. However, there was something about his greeting that made it easy for her to speak to him and, in no time at all, they were engaged in an animated conversation. He let her have her say, as she held forth about her beliefs, and as she attempted to put this Jew in his place. When she had finished, he spoke to her, and he obviously read her heart because his words hit home, as she ran off to bring her friends to meet him. She obviously had listened also. If she had kept up the confrontation nothing would have happened. We often see this on television when two or more of a panel are speaking at the same time, and nobody is listening, and the whole debate descends into a shouting match. There is a story told about two deaf men who met on the road. One asked the other, 'Are you going fishing?' 'No, I'm going fishing', was the answer. 'Ah, that's alright, I thought that maybe you might be going fishing.' A good example of non-communication!

We are all familiar with the kind of person that makes us afraid to ask them how they are, because they'll tell us! They are moaners and, even if they are not suffering from depression, they are carriers! A little bit of common sense is needed here. They need somebody to listen, but they themselves never listen, and their story never changes. Sometimes, listening to them is enabling them to continue the moaning. I may not be so readily available to such people, unless I am prepared to challenge them to move to other areas of their lives, or to speak about something or someone else for a change. Our listening could possibly divert some of the self-preoccupation, even though this is unlikely. We should not give up on them, however, because they are often very lonely people, badly in need of a 'visit' from someone. 'I was in prison, and you came to visit me', says Jesus; and when his listeners asked him when that happened, he replied 'Whatever you did to the least of these, that is what you did onto me.' Spending time, listening, to such people, is like visiting someone in prison, and if I remember this, it can help me to give them the time.

What I am saying here is that listening is a ministry. It is a way of Christian service. The ideal of Christianity is to be Christ to everyone, and to see Christ in everyone. This is certainly not easy, and I sometimes wonder how the Father can see Christ in some people! There is a pattern in this. I begin by trying to be Christ to others. After a while, I come to know the other ('She's very nice when you get to know her'), and then it becomes possible to see Christ in her. There would be little merit if I could see Christ straightaway. The human soul is like a deep deep well with a gurgling spring of living water at the bottom. Unfortunately, the well is filled with the wreckage of life, and the water cannot reach the top. *Kenosis* is the Greek word for conversion, which literally means to *empty out.* Conversion is a process of emptying that wreckage, so that the gurgling waters can reach the top and overflow into the lives of others. Beneath the driest desert there is plenty of water, but it cannot reach the surface, except in very rare places. To be a good listener goes a long way towards enabling another unburden a lot of this human wreckage. The topic of conversation, of course, doesn't have to be heavy, to demand positive listening from us, because it is in the mundane everyday conversations that we learn to listen. 'They that are faithful in little things shall be faithful in great things also.' It is a disposition, a way of being, a way of serving.

Joy

In a beautiful story about a young boy called Willie Juan, we are told that Jesus, as the Medicine Man, gave him a small jar of oil and told him to rub three drops on his heart, before the Medicine Man could do anything for him. The first drop was forgiveness of others, the second was acceptance of self, and the third was called joy. I remember when I heard the story first I was puzzled by the inclusion of joy as something we were able to *do*. I had thought of it as an emotion and, if things were good, we experienced it, and if things were bad, it was absent. I had never thought of joy as being a decision. It was only when I came to accept love as a decision that I was able to see the broader picture.

When I speak with couples in preparation for marriage, I stress that love is much more than a feeling. I would be concerned about a couple getting married because they feel love for each other. Of course, they feel love, but it must be much more than that. Feelings don't last, they tend to come and go, to ebb and flow. I cannot control feelings, which are far too elusive to build a whole life on. I cannot guarantee that I will feel the same tomorrow about anything. I can, however, control decisions, and I can renew a decision each morning. The fact that the decision is accompanied by a feeling, that is a bonus, but it is not a prerequisite. It is the same with joy. This is a decision that I make for others.

To say that it is a decision I make for others could imply that it is phony, because it is contrived. I don't think so. Experience has shown that those who make this decision for others are joyful people. My goodwill is confirmed by the fact that, even if I am exhausted, and I feel that I have little to offer others, once I make a decision for joy for others, I soon experience a real joy. That may sound strange to those who have never tried it, so I am writing this in the hope that some of my readers might find out for themselves. As a teacher, I have often entered a classroom on Monday morning, not exactly full of the joys of living. However, I found that, if I made a decision for joy for the sake of others at nine o' clock, I really did feel joyful by ten. If, on the other hand, I did not make that decision, I was not pleasant to be around one hour later!

I cannot write about joy without reference to those people who have no reason to be joyful. There is an enormous amount of suffering in today's world, and there are millions suffering from the cruelties and injustices of others. It is not too realistic to speak about joy to such unfortunates. My heart goes out to them and, indeed, when I think of them, I could easily feel guilty speaking about joy at all. However, I have to avoid allowing such thoughts paralyse me into inactivity, into doing or saying nothing. I don't think I would be helping these people if I ignored all those who are not so oppressed, because I look to those others to make positive and definite contributions towards alleviating the condition of the poor, the oppressed, and the marginalised. To allow myself be determined by the condition of so many, without reference to those who are not so oppressed, would preclude my writing about Humility, Gratitude, Hope, etc.

As I said earlier, I cannot allow myself be frozen into inactivity in the face of the hopelessness of some situations. It is a tragedy, of course, that half the world should be dying of hunger, while the other half is on a diet to get down the weight. There are several services available to help those with marriage difficulties, but what I like particularly about something like Marriage Encounter, is that it is there to make good marriages better. If there is no such service available, then more and more people will end up with the counsellors. I would prefer to be guided by a lighthouse, than to be rescued by a lifeboat.

The joy of which I speak is not some sort of tidal wave of exuberance, but a quiet, gentle, and contagious sense of well-being. It shows itself when I am happy to meet someone, and that person knows it. It shows itself when I show an interest in the project of a child, or the experience of a young person in a new job. It is an expression of interest in another, because joy is not something I can keep to myself; it must go out to others. It is not something I can easily disguise, no more than most people fail to disguise sadness. It evokes a response in another, even if that response is annoyance from someone who epitomises the idea of misery loving company! The sense of joy that is transmitted enhances sharing, companionship, and each and every expression of love. It is said that God loves a cheerful giver. It is doing something with a smile. It costs nothing, and it is highly contagious. 'I thank my God each time I think of you, and when I pray for you, I pray with joy.' It is about going about my work willingly, and being pleasant in my dealings with others. We speak of a doctor with a bad bedside manner, or of officials being gruff, grumpy, and unsociable. It is uplifting to meet someone with a smile, and with a pleasant disposition.

I have spoken of those who are the victims of cruelty and injustice. I can do something about that by staying at home, and starting at home. In my own little way, I can become part of the solution. I certainly am not contributing to that cruelty and injustice in my dealings with others. It can be my way of making some reparation for the boorishness, thoughtlessness, and selfishness of others.

It is interesting to notice adults dealing with babies, or very young children. There is generally a deliberate effort to be cheerful, to play games, to evoke a smile. It is as if it is the only form of communication the baby understands, or responds to. I am not suggesting that we behave like that in our dealings with adults, but we certainly could lighten up a little, and avoid being serious all the time. Even when I am serious, I can be joyful, as against being morose and solemn.

My most familiar image of Jesus, as he walked the roads of Galilee, is one of a vibrant person, with distinctive features, and a sparkle in his eye. He may not always have been smiling but, through his healing and his teaching, he was bringing enormous joy to many. It must have been that smile that attracted the children. They would most certainly have shied away otherwise. It is obvious that he was particularly attractive in his personality, and it is reasonable to assume that this was bubbly, lively, and vivacious. He came that we should have life, and have it to the full. He was filled with the Spirit. He rejoiced in that Spirit, as he prayed out aloud to the Father. 'From sad and solemn saints, O Lord deliver us,' is a prayer I often heard as a child. Such people do not inspire, and are more likely to depress. We think of heaven as a state of eternal joy, so it is reasonable to assume that those who live the life of the blessed would be brimming over with joy, and filled with life. I never concern myself about life after death. I am, however, concerned to ensure that there is sufficient life before death. Everybody dies, but not everybody lives. Some people settle for existing and, when they die it is necessary to have a doctor certify that fact, because there is not much external difference! One could write on their tomb-stones, 'Died at forty, buried at eighty.' The person was dead for years, while still walking around.

We sometimes forget that joy is one of the fruits of the Spirit. The Spirit brings the gifts and, when I avail of them, I produce the fruits. There is a story in the gospel of a tree in full bloom with leaves but with no fruit, so Jesus cursed it and it withered. There are several parables about the servants being held responsible for the talents or the gifts entrusted to them. They were expected to make use of them, and to produce a return. I believe that joy is something that God has a right to expect from us. It certainly should be evident in the life of a Christian. Because of Jesus' resurrection, his followers are expected to be witnesses of joy, hope, and on-going celebration. We often hear it said that many of our liturgies are devoid of joy, and more appropriate to commemorating Jesus' death than his resurrection, and triumphant return in glory. 'The choirs of heaven ring out their joy,' we are told in the psalms. When our church singing is joyful, it is more fitting a celebration. Hope in resurrection even permits us have joyful funeral liturgies.

It may seem strange when I say that joy is something serious. What I mean by that is that it is not something I can take or leave. It is one of the marks of the Christian. As we watch a football game, we experience the enormous explosion of joy and delight from a section of the fans, when their team scores a goal. It is something quite evident and tangible. It is not something disguised, or hidden under a bushel. I can share joy with others, as if passing on a lit candle to them. One of my own favourite prayers in the morning is, 'Lord, may your Spirit within me touch the hearts of those I meet today, either through the words I say, the prayers I pray, the life I live, or the very person that I am.' Let us turn to the Spirit now:

Spirit and breath of God, please enkindle within me the spark of joy. Release your joy in my heart, so that it might flow out into the lives of others. May my gratitude be expressed with great joy, and let me be a leaven for uplifting joy wherever I go. May your joy be always in my heart.

Forgiveness

To sin is human, to forgive is divine. The reflections in this book are intended as helps to living the Christian life more fully. One of the greatest obstacles to enjoying the fullness of life is to have an unforgiving heart. The whole story of salvation is about how God forgives, and this is held up to us as being a core quality of divine love. To share in that life is to share in that love. Yes, indeed, to forgive is divine. I have come across people who speak about how difficult it is for them to forgive someone for the hurt inflicted on them. It is always necessary to impress upon such people that forgiveness is something we can do only by the grace of God.

The human heart is not a forgiving heart, as we see when we consider how many people find it almost impossible to forgive themselves. If Jesus had died in any other way than being nailed to a cross, the cross is still a very good way of representing Christian living. The vertical, downward, bar represents what comes from God to us, and the horizontal bar represents us going out to others. In other words, what comes down from God must go out to others, or it ceases to come from God. If forgiveness comes from God to us, it is so that forgiveness might flow from us to others. If we refuse to forgive, we are not forgiven. 'Forgive, and you shall be forgiven ...' In the one prayer that Jesus taught us, he put us on the spot when he asked us to pray that God might forgive us as we forgive others.

For those of us brought up in the Catholic Church, an undue emphasis was placed on the sacrament of Confession as a means of forgiveness. This was seen as some sort of magic formula that worked automatically, irrespective of whether we had forgiveness in our hearts for others, or not. It is now called the sacrament of Reconciliation, and this implies more than just forgiveness.

Once again, I repeat that all of this is the work of the Spirit. By myself, I do not have what it takes to live the Christian life.

Spirit and breath of God, please give me a forgiving heart. Rid my heart of all unforgiveness, and give me the strength to let go of my resentments, my need to get even, and my need to prove that I am right. Please give me the humility to open my hands with generosity, and to let go of all that wounded pride.

Unforgiveness is a real cancer in the spirit. It blocks healing, and it comes in the way of inner peace. It is a dis-ease that can effect my health, and my sense of well-being. There is a wonderful freedom in forgiveness, where I free the other person, and I release myself from the prison of resentment and wounded pride. All of this resentment can be very absorbing, and it can be on my mind during every waking hour. It is with me night and day, and it effects my moods. When I have a resentment against another, it is as if I were drinking poison and I'm expecting the other person to die! It requires a generous spirit to be able to forgive, but the rewards are worth it.

As a Christian, of course, I have no choice. Being a Christian does not mean that I become some sort of door-mat, without feelings, and that others can walk all over me, and I am not supposed to feel hurt, angry, or resentful. I will, of course, feel all of the above, but the Spirit of God will lead me out of those feelings into a freedom that only those who experience it can understand.

Jesus came to show us how to live. He was God-among-us, going from place to place, in search of sinners, to assure them that forgiveness was theirs for the asking. He said he had not come to condemn anyone, but to seek and to find the lost. In effect, he is saying that the Father is looking for every opportunity to forgive, and to welcome back those who have strayed away. He told stories to illustrate this point, and his preferential option for being in the company of sinners was a clear declaration of this message. With his dying words, he is asking forgiveness for those who are killing him. He certainly has placed forgiveness very much in the center of the life of a Christian. Forgiveness is what keeps love alive. Imagine a couple kneeling in front of me to get married. They may not have a great deal of sense, and even less money, but their love will last if they have enough forgiveness in their hearts. When I was growing up, my father killed a pig once a year, to feed all of us who were never hungry, but, according to us at the time, we were always starving! This was before we had fridges and deep-freezers, so the only way he could prevent the bacon from going bad was to pack it in salt. That did the trick, and I never knew of bacon that went off. I now think of that salt as the forgiveness that is a preservative for love. Love that is packaged in forgiveness will continue to be healthy and life-giving.

Forgiveness is needed on every side. Guilt is quite prevalent, where people are unable or unwilling to forgive themselves. A leading psychiatrist told me that he could send one third of his patients home from all the psychiatric hospitals in his area, if he could get them to deal with their guilt which, he added, is caused mostly by religion. What a travesty, that the message of Jesus should be used to lay guilt-trips on people. We certainly can have remorse, and we may well have to make amends, but there comes a time when we should be able to let go of the guilt, learn the lesson from the experience, and move on, much wiser. 'Lord, give me the serenity to accept the things I cannot change … ' I have known people who went to Confession, sought and received forgiveness from God, and still refused to forgive themselves. There are people who may also need to forgive God for something they believe he allowed happen to them. Their poor self-image, their sense of worthlessness, or of inadequacy, may imply that God treated them less favourably than others. They somehow got a dumb deal in life, and they feel that God has been less than generous with them. Others experience great tragedy, and they cannot understand why God did not intervene to prevent this happening. I have come across many people, and their first reaction to a tragedy is to fall out with God. God is usually allowed back into favour eventually, however, but it involves forgiving him, or conceding that he had nothing to do with what happened, or he saw the possibility of a better good. While I would question why God should have such involvement attributed to him, I can well understand why people should feel this way.

At the beginning of the last chapter, I spoke of the story of Willie Juan and the Medicine Man. The Medicine Man gave him some oil, and told him to rub three drops on his heart that night, so that the Spirit of the Medicine Man could begin to effect great changes in his life. It is significant that the first drop was forgiveness of others. In my own experience of praying with others in the whole area of healing, I find that I have to spend quite a lot of time exploring the possibility of there being unforgiveness within the heart of the person being prayed with. I always consider this to be a serious barrier to the work of God's healing in our lives. Just to make a point: I might spend a few sessions exploring with the person the areas of unforgiveness, and praying for the willingness to forgive, and maybe only one session praying for healing. The forgiveness, of course, involves real healing anyhow. I think of the Lord healing from the inside out. He heals the unforgiveness, the resentments, the angers, and the guilt in the heart first, and then he heals the body. 'Your sins are forgiven, arise and walk.' I could never imagine a blind man being healed of his blindness, and going down the road filled with resentment towards another. That man is still blind, and has not been healed. We are told that 'the man followed Jesus down the road, praising and glorifying God'.

I will finish with a prayer, because I feel that this is absolutely essential if I am ever going to be able to have a forgiving heart.

Spirit and breath of God, I ask you please, as you live in my heart, to sow within me the seeds of forgiveness. Generate in me a deep and constant desire to forgive, and to be a forgiving person. Continue to form me in the image of Jesus, so that my heart may be as forgiving as his.

Service

St James tells us that faith without good works is dead. Christianity is about a person, Jesus, about faith in him, and following him. This means that it must always lead us into action, because 'Jesus went about doing good.' His life was more than just preaching and teaching. He came 'to do and to teach'. He washed feet himself, before he asked his followers to do the same. He fed the hungry, he healed the sick, he freed those in bondage, and he raised the dead. He was constantly on the go, and he was always at the service of others.

There is one occasion in the gospel that appeals to me more than most. Jesus and his disciples were tired, and the crowds continued to follow them. Jesus felt sorry for his disciples, and he felt sorry for those that followed him. He told his disciples to go away and rest, and that he would stay back and dismiss the crowd. I am sure there were many many times when he must have been exhausted in his ministry, and yet he was always ready to draw on some reserve of energy to minister to others.

In Matthew 25 we get a preview of the General Judgement. Those who are declared worthy of entering the kingdom are those who fed the hungry, clothed the naked, welcomed the stranger, and visited those in prison. It might shock some religious people to discover that the questions asked are scandalously materialistic. The people are not asked anything about church attendance, prayer, or spiritual experiences. They are asked about a piece of bread, a cup of water, and an item of clothing. This is not to denigrate the religious dimension, but to emphasise, once again, that faith without good works is dead. As in a previous reflection, I emphasise that the cross is a very fitting symbol for a properly balanced religious practice. Some people have a religion that is purely vertical, that concerns themselves and God, without reference to others. They are so busy praying that they haven't time to help others. The priest and the Levite, who passed the traveller who was beaten up on the road to Jericho, are a very good example of this. The Pharisees themselves were very much like that. There are others whose practice of religion is very much horizontal, where it has to do with myself and others, without any great reference to God. It is a kind of philanthropy, a form of do-goodism, where the emphasis is on action, without a contemplative dimension. The conflict between the active and contemplative life is an age-old one, and it is difficult to get the balance right. But for a proper Christian life, it is necessary to correct any imbalance. What comes from God to me must go out to others. Jesus came to serve others, and he told his disciples to do the same. The cross-over between the vertical and the horizontal, makes it easier for us to understand the proper emphasis in the Christian message.

One of the concepts that puzzle some people is the idea that inspires contemplative religious life. On a human level, it doesn't make a lot of sense, and may even be seen as a waste of a life, or an attempt by someone to avoid the hardships of worldly living. It is difficult to see what it produces at the end of the day and, certainly under the heading of service, it is questioned. The religious who run schools or hospitals are seen to be providing a worthwhile service, but with the contemplative life, this is not so evident. There are many ways of providing a service. 'They also serve who only stand and wait,' the poet tells us. Contemplative life is a life spent in the service of God, and of humanity. It is service in the fullest sense of that word. Through prayer, it is spent worshipping God, while it is also spent in praying for the rest of us. Who knows what disasters would come upon the world were it not for the prayers of such people. Jean Vanier says that some of the greatest movements for good in the history of the world are brought about by the quiet prayers of totally unknown people. This is a selfless service, and it is authentic service, in that it is given without seeking a reward. I referred to the General Judgement earlier. In that scenario as described by Jesus, those who were people of service are surprised to discover that this is acknowledged because, for them, it was a way of being, and they could not conceive of any other kind of living. Being of service becomes second nature after a while, and we are all familiar with people who demonstrate this in their lives.

'Constant thought of others' is something that we all could develop. It is something that must be developed, while depending on the Spirit in our hearts to inspire this action. Jesus said that the Spirit would remind us because, quite often, we can be guilty of thoughtlessness. It is not that we are against giving a helping hand, but that we just don't think of it at the time.

Spirit and breath of God, please inspire me with a spirit of service to others. Please remind me, and give me a thoughtful heart. I pray that your presence within me might be a source of inspiration for me in my availability, and my willingness to serve others.

The idea of Christian service becomes something quite serious when we remember that Jesus takes anything done for others as being done for him. He identifies himself with others, especially with the marginalised and the outcast ('the least of these my brothers'). It is an extraordinary privilege that is extended to each of us, to think that we can actually serve Jesus in person, when we serve others. Those of the horizontal emphasis on religion might attach great importance to keeping Jesus company in the Blessed Sacrament, and forget that they also can keep him company in the hospital ward, or by the kitchen fire. The ideal of Christianity is to see Christ in others, and to be Christ to others. It may not be easy to see Christ in some people, but in this lies the test of our faith, and the depth of our Christian service. Our service is tested when we get no recognition, and no return. It is difficult to continue the service in such circumstances, but this is precisely where Christian service differs from all other forms of service. 'To give and not to count the cost ... to serve and not to seek reward ...' Only those who have a clear mental impression of the level of service shown in the life of Jesus, can have any hope of providing unselfish service. It is very natural to be selfish, and any of us can be like this, without being aware of it. It is only by opening my heart of the workings of the Spirit that I can have any hope of being able to serve others with an unselfish heart.

The Christ in us wants to minister to the Christ in others. Sometimes it is the resurrected Christ ministering to the wounded Christ. In AA, which is based on one alcoholic helping another, it is a question of sharing in the empathy that Jesus had as he joined us on our human journey. He knew what it was like to be rejected, to be misunderstood, to be an outcast. He knew what it was like to be tired, lonely, hungry, or homeless. He brought all of that to his ministry, and this was shown by his patience, his tolerance, and his understanding. There is a great loneliness in suffering when others around us have no idea of what we are going through. If I have stitches up my chest from a heart by-pass, I am more likely to get sympathy and understanding than if I were suffering from depression. It is difficult to see the inner hurts. Jesus could see the wounded heart, and he could minister to the troubled mind, or the fearful spirit. He can do all of that, and he wants to continue doing all of that through us. The Holy Spirit came to complete the work of Jesus. The Spirit does that in and through us. When Jesus ascended into heaven, he brought the body he had with him. He sent down his Spirit, and he asks us to provide the body. A spirit by itself cannot do anything. The evil spirit needs somebody's tongue to tell the lie, or somebody's hand to prime the bomb. It is the same with the Holy Spirit. We provide the hands, feet, and voice, and Jesus continues his ministry to others through us. 'Make me a channel of your peace ... Where there is hunger, let me bring your food ...' The horizontal emphasis on religion could have us doing all we can to get to heaven. The Christian is someone who believes that heaven has already been earned, and the Christian vocation has much more to do with getting heaven down here. I often think it is much more difficult to get heaven into people than to get people into heaven! St Paul tells us that our salvation depends on what Jesus has done, and on our willingness to accept that fact. I believe that, to the extent that we believe that we are saved, and that heaven is ours, we are much more inclined to give our attention to getting heaven down here. Our religious practice can easily become very selfish, and selfishness is most insidious when it is disguised as religion.

Jesus asks us to take up his cross and follow him. I think that the cross is not too well understood. Someone loses a job, another person gets a stroke, a family member dies, and any of these things can be referred to as a cross. I do not accept that, because these things happen to non-Christians as well. Many of these things are not blessings, whereas the cross is always a source of blessing. When I decide to follow Jesus in Christian service, then everything I do as a result of that decision is a cross. It is easy, and it is light, as Jesus said it would be, because people of service are the happiest people in the world. If you want to get someone to do something for you, ask a busy person. Some people are so busy doing nothing, that they haven't time for anyone. I remember speaking about saints to a primary school class one time, when one of the boys told me that his granny was a saint. I asked him why he said that, and he told me that he heard his mother say this, because his granny always had time for everyone. I told him that, even though I did not know his granny, she certainly was a saint if that could have been said about her.

Spirit and breath of God, please help us to have time for others. Give us a spirit of generosity with our time and talents, so that others might benefit, as we do what we can to extend heaven to those we meet. May your presence within me touch the hearts of those I meet, either through the words I say, the prayers I pray, the life I live, or the very person that I am.

Time

I believe that we could benefit greatly by having a fairly realistic concept of time. Time is something that is always passing, yet is ever present and, while we use it, or waste it, we may not give any serious consideration to it. The only time that actually exists is now, because the past is gone and the future hasn't arrived yet. It is difficult to live in the now, because it is so easy for us to be stuck in the past, with guilt, angers, regrets, and hindsights, or in the future, with worries, anxieties, and dread. God is totally a God of now, ('I am who am'), and I will never meet God until I become a person of now. Many people will not meet God until they die, and can no longer run away into a time that does not exist. Living in the present takes quite a long time to achieve. Old habits die hard, and when we have spent years all over the place, it can be quite difficult to gather all of our resources into the now, the only place where life is to found. We have often heard it said of somebody, 'Oh, he's all over the place. She badly needs to get herself together. He's very scattered.' The opposite to that is to be together, to be whole, wholesome, or, to use another word, to be holy.

The only value the past has are the lessons it taught me. I would be a very wise person today if I learned every lesson that life taught me. Jesus asks the leading question 'Who do you say that I am?' If he is Saviour, then my past is in his hands, for forgiveness, for healing, and for redemption. Jesus takes my past, garners the nuggets of wisdom from it, entrusts those to me, and then blows the rest away. If I entrust my past to Jesus as Saviour, then I have no business being back there trying to relive it. 'Lord, give me the serenity to accept the things I cannot change ...' Yesterday went away at midnight, and it will never come back. There is nothing I can do to change it. I met someone yesterday whose son was killed in an accident, and she was riddled with guilt and regret over all the things she had not said, and all the things she had not done. Guilt is always part of bereavement because, no matter how much we did for the person who has died, there will always be something else we should have done, or something else we ought to have said. The hard fact is that those occasions will never return. What I can do, however, is learn from my regrets, and make use of the time I have with those who still remain. My regrets for the past can help make me much more sensitive in the present. 'All things work together for good for those who love God ...' God never wastes a thing. That is why it is important that I make full use of the past to enrich the present. Any compassion I have has come out of that room of my past, where my own brokenness has taught me that I cannot afford to look down my nose at anyone else. I am a product of that room, and it is important that I allow Jesus into it, to redeem it, to free me from any bondage there, to heal the brokenness, to forgive the sin, and to entrust to me the nuggets of wisdom that experience has taught. Experience is a very good school, even if the fees are often very high. It would be a great tragedy to waste the wisdom of experience.

Some people spend a lot of their time worrying about the future. Once again, we are faced with that question from Jesus, 'Who do you say that I am?' If Jesus is Lord, then why should I worry about the future? I need not worry what the future holds, if I believe that he holds the future. Instead of trying to anticipate the wheelchair, the cancer ward, or the cardiac unit, it is better to come back out of that room of my future, to allow Jesus take up residence there, and to accept my life in twenty-four segments each morning. When I woke up this morning, I went on my knees, and thanked God for the gift of today. It is pure free gift, and there are many who did not get the gift of today. Because it is gift, maybe that is why it is called the present. Written on the gift are the words 'batteries included'! Because each day is provided with its daily bread, there is nothing going to happen today that the Lord and myself will not be able to handle. I do not know how many days there are in the room of my future, but I know that Jesus knows, and so I accept each new day from him, knowing that, even if this is my last day, the grace to live that day comes with the day. Time is a gift from God, and when I am prepared to accept it as a gift, I will appreciate it all the more.

If I am willing to accept Jesus as Saviour of the room of my past, and Lord of the room of my future, then I am prepared to live in the room of today, where Jesus is God. I must remember that there is nothing impossible for God. It is in the now that salvation, life, and happiness are to be found. Every now lived well makes up a full life. It is so easy to waste the present moment, if I am going to do something 'later on,' 'some other time,' or 'when I get a chance'. Of course, I cannot possibly do everything right now, but procrastination is the thief of time. All diets begin next Monday! There are people who cannot see why they should do something today, when they can put it off till to-morrow. When I appreciate the gift of time, I become more willing to be responsible for the gift, and to make full use of it. A full and wholesome future is concealed within the kernel of now, and every moment of now is but a foretaste of eternity. 'I shall pass this way but once. Any good deed that I can do, any good word that I can say, let me do it now, let me say it now, because I will never pass this way again.' We speak about passing time, killing time, biding our time, and saving time. Studies in the workplace involve time and motion studies, where an attempt is made

to maximise the use of time, and of activity, in order to
achieve maximum returns. 'Time and tide wait for no one.'
'Now is the acceptable time, today is the day of salvation.'

Jesus was obviously very conscious of time. He advises
his followers to make full use of the present, because the
time will come when they will not have the opportunities
they have now. 'Be alert, because you do not know when
the time will come.' 'You did not recognise the time when
God came to save you ...' 'The time is coming when all the
dead will hear my voice ...' He was constantly calling on
them to act in the now. Bartimeus, the blind man, sat by
the roadside, and he was told that Jesus of Nazareth was
passing by. He had a choice of seizing the moment, and
being healed, or of letting it go, and remaining a blind
man. There is such a thing as a moment of grace. 'There is
a tide in the affairs of man which, taken at its tide, leads on
to greatness ...' says Shakespeare. Because time is fleeting,
it calls for action right now, and in that is the moment of
grace. That is what I mean when I speak of God being a
God of now. In my list of sins, as a child, I spoke of 'sins of
omission', while not understanding too well what that
meant. I can understand that today, and I see the times
when I had 'to look into something,' or 'to give some
thought to that,' as times when I was buying time, as we
call it. In other words, it could easily lead to sins of omission, because the good never gets done, and the moment
of grace is neglected. I believe that I will be held accountable for my use of time. It is a very precious commodity,
and it should be given some sort of sacred status. Each
moment is filled with opportunity, and every hour is a gift
of God. I myself celebrate eucharist each morning with a
group of very elderly people in a retirement home. From
day to day I notice how individuals are slipping from
alertness to confusion, from an armchair to a wheelchair,
from self-sufficiency to dependence. I have a daily reminder
of the transience of time. Their journey is irreversible, as

they move into another time in their lives. Soon time will become eternity, and all clocks and calendars dispensed with. I consider it a wonderful privilege to minister to them at this stage of their lives and, through my own reflection on what I witness, I myself am enriched greatly in my appreciation of the gift of time. 'For time it is a precious thing, and time brings all things to an end. Time, with all its labour, along with all its joys, let no man steal away your time' is to paraphrase the words of a song.

Let us end with a prayer.

Spirit and breath of God, please give us a deep reverence for the gift of time. Help us avail of the present moment, for the moment of grace that it is. Inspire us with a deep appreciation of the now, and to be people of action in using the now. Please help us not to waste time, but to treasure it as a very precious gift from God, that is given to me for others. As time ticks by, please remind me to be more conscious of the fact that it is bringing me along a journey into eternity, when time will no longer mean anything.

Compassion

Compassion means to align oneself with the hurts or sufferings of another. It is like unscrewing the top of another's head, and looking out through that person's eyes, in an attempt to see things the way the other person sees them. It is more than empathy, and much more than sympathy. It is joining another in her suffering, and sharing the pain with her. We speak of Christ's suffering as his passion. Com-passion is uniting one's struggles to that of another, and accompanying that person on the way of the cross. It is very much part of the mission of Jesus. He came to share the journey with us, and to let us know that we are not alone. Compassion entails letting another know that he is not alone. It is being there for others. Accompanying others is a very real form of ministry. It is to be a Simon of Cyrene for some other Christ, as that person struggles with the cross.

Jesus had a compassionate heart. This is evident again and again. It is seen at its clearest when he wept over Jerusalem, or when he wept at the tomb of Lazarus. He had so much love in his heart, and it really hurt him deeply to see his beloved Jerusalem refusing the gift of God, because he knew what suffering this would bring upon it later. For a number of years, I brought groups to the Holy Land. On the first morning, we normally went up to the Mount of Olives. From there we walked down a path that led to the Garden of Gethsemani below. On the way down we stopped off at a little church that is built in the shape of a tear. It is called the Dominus Flevit church, because it was here that Jesus sat as he wept over

Jerusalem. There is a large glass window behind the altar and, during Mass, as you looked at the altar, you could also see across the Kedron valley and the old city of Jerusalem. It is really striking to recall the words of Jesus at that moment. 'Salvation was within your grasp, but you would not accept it. Now your enemies will surround you on every side, and your temple will be left without one stone upon another.'

The thought of Jesus crying over Jerusalem gives us some insight into his heart. His words are words of compassion, and not words of condemnation. Any one of us can well imagine what might be going on in the mind and heart of Jesus as he looks into the spirit of any one of us. Because his message is one of love, he is sad that love should not be accepted. His motives are pure. He has no hidden agenda. We are the ones who benefit from his love. Unrequited love is a difficult cross to bear. In a way, it could well have been more painful than the nails. Grief is the price to be paid for love. If I don't want to cry at a funeral, then I shouldn't love anyone. Jesus had an extraordinary capacity for love; therefore he must have shed many a tear.

Jesus loved Lazarus, and his sisters Martha and Mary. He was in the habit of going to spend some time with them on occasions. They may have provided him with a safe haven, where he could rest for a while, from his arduous labours. He was told that Lazarus was sick and, for some reason, he did not rush to his side. He then told his disciples that Lazarus was dead, and he left immediately to be with Martha and Mary. (I cannot understand why he had not gone there earlier, but that is not part of our present reflection.) His very arrival created a stir, and Martha and Mary rushed to meet him. Martha told him that if he had been there her brother would not have died. When Jesus spoke about being the source of resurrection, Martha accepted his word. He then accompanied the two sisters to the tomb. This is the accompaniment I spoke of earlier. When he got to the tomb, he even joined them with his tears. This was real compassion, which was Jesus' way of expressing his love at that time. No wonder the onlookers remarked, 'See how he loved him.' Here we have the two sides of love. In his heart he loved them, and by his actions, he showed that love. Compassion is love in action.

Once again, we have to remind ourselves that having a compassionate heart is a direct result of the work of the Spirit within us.

Spirit and breath of God, please give me a heart full of compassion for others. Help me to feel their pain, and to walk the way of the cross with them. Please give me enough love to want to spend time with them, to listen to them, and to share their burden. Give me a listening ear, a willing hand, an available shoulder, and a loving heart, so that I might be open to bringing the love of Jesus to those I meet on the road of life.

Even as I write this, I am hoping and praying that something I say might serve as a healing balm to someone who reads it. We can all exercise compassion towards others, if we have the goodwill to do so. It is always a question of goodwill. I don't have to go out in search of those who are hurting. When I have the right disposition, and the willingness to help, the Lord will send people to me. I need never doubt this. The Lord entrusts certain gifts and talents to me. All of these are given to me to be used in the service of others. I myself never discover my own talents. If I do, I am like someone at a party who insists on singing, and he's the only one there who thinks he can sing! On the other hand, there could be somebody else at the same party, and everybody is calling on him to sing. He had better pay attention, because this is the way the Lord tells us what gift he has given us. If people call on me for a shoulder to cry on, for a listening ear, or for a helping hand, this is clear evidence from God as to what gifts and talents he has entrusted to me. At the end of time, as we are clearly

told in the gospels, I will have to render an account of how
I used those talents. I believe there is compassion within
the heart of every person and, of course, there must be
compassion within the heart of the Christian. That is why
there is such revulsion at the atrocities perpetuated by
some people upon others. We have had mass murders,
child molestations, and even genocide. What revolts us
most, I believe, is that it is difficult for us to believe how an
ordinary human being could possibly do this. How can
such a person sleep at night, or relate to others in a normal
way? It is seen as a perversion, as a total corruption of the
human spirit. It is frightening when we see the complete
breakdown of the moral fibre of humanity. I believe we
were created to love, and we can only have peace when we
fulfill our mission in life.

While fully accepting the role of God's Spirit in sowing
the seeds, and cultivating the growth of compassion within
our hearts, I believe that it is up to us to practise this virtue
on every occasion we can. This is something I can nurture
and develop. I myself may not notice any significant improvement, but this is unimportant. It is important, however, that others notice the improvement. It is like holiness.
If I myself notice that I am getting very holy, then it is very
suspect! I'll leave the discovering to others, and if they
choose to tell me what they notice, it will give me a smile,
because I have to live with me, and I know only too well
what I'm like! I get thousands of opportunities every day
to exercise compassion. It is in the little things that the
practice is strengthened. To become faithful in little things,
leads on to fidelity in greater things. Like giving affirmation, and engaging in Christian service, it will become a
way of life for me after a while, and I will exercise compassion without being aware of it.

To have a compassionate heart will lead to suffering, as
I share the pain of others. I will be deeply upset by the
swollen bellies of those children in Ethiopia, or the piles of

rotten corpses discovered in the refugee camp. I will not be able to switch channels, or to turn over the page, when I do not like what I see. I will no longer be able to run away but, as far as my suffering brothers and sisters are concerned, I am here to stay. To be compassionate is to be here for the long haul. There are no quick-fixes for the things which disturb me. I will always have somebody or something pulling at my heart strings. Christian compassion is not a nine-to-five job, where I can switch off, and leave it all aside until tomorrow. On the other hand, it does not mean that I am always and ever complaining, scolding, or lecturing; nor that I am always in despair, and unable to enjoy life because others are in misery. 'Lord, give me the serenity to accept the things I cannot change, courage to change the things I can, and the wisdom to know the difference.' The most I can hope to do for others is to heal sometimes, to help often, and to care always. I cannot always heal, nor am I always the best person who can help. Others may not be ready or willing to be healed, and they may not seek or desire my help. I must always avoid the danger of playing God and trying to fix things for others. It is here that the Spirit gives me the sensitivity to discern what I should do. If I am led by the Spirit, then my compassion will always be sensitive, discreet, and uplifting. It will free both me and those towards whom it is directed.

Spirit and breath of God, please imbue my heart with a gentle and sensitive spirit. Loving others with compassion is essentially your work. Make me a channel of your peace, your love, and your compassion. Let me be a pipe or a conduit, through which your love flows, rather than a generator or transformer which controls your power. I say 'yes' to you, and I trust you to complete the process within my heart.

Discipline

When I speak of discipline, I speak of something that flows from the concept of being a disciple. It is not boot camp, French Foreign Legion stuff, where the crack of the whip is my biggest influence. It is about an ordered life that is based on decisions, where there is some plan and purpose, and where self-will is not running the show. It is sad to see a life where self-will has run riot. The person is no longer in control, and the demons within, like the flock of pigs in the gospel story, will drive that person over the edge into destruction.

To be entrusted with the gift of life is to accept a serious responsibility. I only get one shot at it, and there are no dress rehearsals. Indeed, life is too precious a gift to be entrusted to any one individual. The risk of getting it all wrong is far too great. I agree with being given the responsibility, but I also agree that I should be held accountable. The welfare of others is deeply effected by my life, whether for good or bad. For every alcoholic, there are about three others whose lives are directly effected by that person's drinking. For every reckless motorist, there are dozens whose lives are in danger.

It is easy to imagine Jesus as someone who led a disciplined, ordered life. Quite often the turmoil in our lives is matched by what is going on within us. Jesus was led by the Spirit, and he never said anything unless the Father told him. He came to do the will of him who sent him, and it is as if he surrendered his will and his life over to the care of his Father. He had to lead his life within very strict boundaries. This would not have been a restriction on

him, because he just would never dream of being anything, or of doing anything that was not within the
Father's will for him. It gave him great joy to do the
Father's will. His life and death were to be the perfect antidote to the sin of disobedience of our first parents.

Theirs was the original sin of indiscipline. They wanted
something, and they went for that, completely disregard-
ing the consequences of their actions. They went for the
immediate satisfaction and gratification, and let the cookie
crumble where it may. To hell with the consequences.
Alcoholics or gamblers are those who take no responsibility
for the outcome of their actions. They have no boundaries,
and, unless the law, or some other outside agent takes over,
they show a recklessness of purpose that is frightening,
and insane. Insane behaviour is to keep repeating the same
action, and to expect a different result on each occasion.

We are told that Jesus went to death because of the
glory that would be his in the future. It was because of
what lay ahead that he faced up to the demands of now. It
was the short-term pain for the long-term gain. He kept
his eyes fixed on the Father and on his mission, just as we
are advised to 'keep your eyes fixed on Jesus, the author
and finisher of our faith,' as we, too, await the glory that
will be ours with him for all eternity. If we are his disciples,
this must impose a discipline. Jesus calls this the cross, and
we take up that cross and carry it whenever we act in con-
formity to his will.

Jesus speaks about prayer and fasting as in the one
breath. By fasting, we restrain the body, and by prayer, we
nurture the spirit. This is a question of attaining the right
balance. Quite often, to speak of indiscipline is to speak of
the body ruling the way we live, either through food,
drink, pleasure, or pampering. There are people who
spend millions trying to glorify the body, through plastic
surgery, or some other kind of artificial stimulant. This is
often an attempt to disguise, if not to prevent, the aging

signs. Of its own accord, the body generally reflects what's going on inside. The smile or the frown tells it all. Discipline has to come from the inside. A healthy mind helps ensure a healthy body. Discipline of the mind contributes greatly to healthy Christian living. It involves ridding the mind of the resentments, the grudges, the angers, and the unforgiveness that can be a real cancer in the spirit. This mindset is very closely aligned with the action of the Spirit within.

> *Spirit and breath of God, please rid my heart of anything that would take from my inner well-being. Fill every corner of my heart with your love, and give me the strength to live with a healthy, loving, and balanced mind. Help me to keep my eyes fixed on Jesus, and the example of his life, and may your gifts direct and sustain me on my journey.*

There are very few problems in life that do not have to do with relationships of one kind or another. I am not getting on too well with another, with myself, or with God. We see the results of not being able to relate to food or to drink, in the lives of those poor unfortunates who suffer from bulimia, anorexia, or alcoholism. All of the compulsions and addictions stem from an inability to relate. Some people cannot relate to money, which becomes a controlling monster that ends up owning its owner. Healthy relationships depend totally on discipline. The sexual drive, without discipline, gives us the horrors of rape, pedophilia, incest, and all the other horrors that result from such a strong drive when out of control. Even within acceptable relationships, the unbridled sexual drive can be very destructive and damaging. It can make one totally unsympathetic to the needs of another, when my needs become a priority at the expense of someone else. This thread of indiscipline creates havoc wherever it emerges. It is obvious then that we cannot speak of love in any way, without a genuine understanding of the centrality of discipline. St Paul says that if we have not love, then we have nothing. Whenever I exercise self-control, I am making more space for those around me. I can take up far too much space in my life and, when I approach, people have to make themselves smaller to make room for me. This is sad, because it is such a travesty. The person without discipline is someone who rides rough-shod over everyone. God help anyone who gets in their way, when they are full flight in pursuit of their self-will and self-gratification.

We usually think of death as something that happens at the end of our lives. Death, however, is much more than that. Death is something that is part of every day we live. Every time I hold back a word, a judgement, or any other kind of verbal or physical violence, I die a little to myself. Death is like a pile of sand at the end of my life, which I can take and sprinkle a little every day as I travel along the way. If I do this, it could happen that there'll be nothing left when I arrive at the end, so I can pass straightaway to ascension. On the other hand, if I leave all the dying until the end, it could well be too late.

I have had the privilege of caring for the terminally ill on many occasions throughout my life. When I came across someone for the first time, I always tried to access how much dying has been done, and how much still needs to be done. Whenever I came across someone who was very troublesome, very demanding, and totally devoid of gratitude, I felt I had a fairly accurate idea of how that life has been spent up till now. When such a person became so weak, and was no longer able to express anger, I have seen that anger in the eyes. It took constant pastoral caring to bring peace to those eyes. On the other hand, I have come across others who were most edifying, and their whole demeanour spoke of a quiet sense of wholeness, of being together, and of accepting each stage of the journey as it happened. They were grateful for everything that was done for them, and I was often asked how I was, before I got that question out of my mouth for them. Such experiences have helped impress on my mind the importance of discipline in our lives. It became a much more important concept for me after seeing it playing such an important role at the hour of death.

Discipline is a very wide umbrella. I cannot hope to cover all the issues and angles here. I can, however, highlight some of the most important issues. Discipline is a Christian quality, and it must be part of the life of anyone who would be a disciple of Jesus. It enhances the quality of life, by giving some sort of structure to that life. It can effect and benefit every area of our lives, even in how we use food, drink, money, and time. It greatly enriches all our relationships, and it enables us to mediate life to others, rather than death. It contributes enormously towards preparing us for the final drama of death and, through the daily dying, or carrying of the cross, it ensures that we share the glory with Jesus for all eternity. It contributes greatly towards responsible living and, because of it, we avoid the havoc that can be created when our self-will runs riot. It enables us have a proper order of priorities, and it enriches our smallest acts. Our discipline with food, drink, sleep, etc., greatly enhances our health and our well-being, and ensures that we live life out to the end, as intended by God. It enables an enormous flow of blessings to enrich our lives, and the sense of satisfaction it provides gives a tranquility and peace of soul that no addiction, compulsion, or riotous appetite could ever hope to match. Indeed, for the person leading a disciplined life, the very thought of addiction, compulsion, or riotous appetite must send a shiver through them, and a deep and grateful appreciation that, however it happened, they did discover that pearl of great price that brought them safe thus far.

Reflection

A life without reflection is not worth living. I always consider that the human mind never gives up during my waking hours, and it must surely have some place in my dreams. We associate dreaming with sleeping, but we can do a lot of day-dreaming while awake. This can be aimless and rudderless sailing, whereas reflection, as I intend using it, is looking at life, examining ideas that enrich the spirit, and communing with that inner spirit by being in touch with feelings, emotions, and thoughts. It involves making constructive use of time, because it helps avoid drifting aimlessly, and being lost in some cloud cuckoo land. It is being in touch with reality, being alert in the present moment, and learning from the unfolding of events in my life. It means harnessing the mind as a source of spiritual nourishment, and it provides food for the soul. I often think of the cow chewing the cud as a symbol of reflection! The cow is regurgitating food already swallowed, is doing this at her ease, and is giving it her full attention. There are many things coming at us in the course of a day, and it is not possible to integrate everything that is worth retaining. In the quiet moments, I can relive a moment, or an event, or something I heard, and the result can be very enriching.

Reflection can take place anywhere. I myself find that walking is a wonderful occasion for reflection and, quite often, after a walk, I can sit here at the computer and write a whole chapter of a book on what was going through my head. Reflection is much more than just thinking. I don't think it can be structured. It is spontaneous up to a point, and yet it needs to be subjected to some slight discipline, to prevent it lapsing into day-dreaming. While I write, I sometimes walk away from my desk, relax in an armchair, go downstairs into my heart, and get in touch with what is happening there. This can and often does lead to a prayer, but this is not necessary, because I consider reflection itself as a form of prayer. I will speak of this later.

For now, I want to look at some of the places which might be more conducive to reflection. I believe that finding a place, and going there, is a prerequisite for reflection. This involves a decision, it is something positive, and it means that I make myself available to this wonderful form of enlightenment and inspiration. There are particular places where I walk that I deliberately choose, because I have found them most conducive to reflection. I love the seaside, and I am fortunate to have easy access to that. This applies all year round, because the calm sea or the angry sea can both have beneficial effects on the human spirit. It is said that spending some time close to an angry sea is an excellent way of ridding oneself of inner turmoil. It is as if the turbulent sea absorbs all the spirit's tensions. In the spring and summer I love to stroll in a public park nearby, where everything around me betokens life. The trees, the flowers, the birds, the insects, and especially the people, are alive, and it is a place where the human spirit can be enlivened.

As I sit at the end of the pier and look out to sea, I am fascinated as I reflect on what is to be seen. I see the horizon, and I know there is much more than that. A graphic reminder of life, and death, which can be just like the horizon. I look at the water, and I realise that I can only see the top of it. There are millions of gallons which I cannot see. The whole place can become a symbol of mystery. I stroll along the beach, which stretches for miles, with its millions and trillions of grains of sand, and I am aware of my own insignificance. I remember walking on the beach one moonlit night. The tide was fully out, and the beach was vast. There was a clear sky overhead, with a beautiful clear moon, and millions of stars. As I stood there, looking around me in awe, I was overcome by a great fear. I am still unsure how much was awe, and how much was fear. In this vast basilica, I felt as small as one of the grains of sand, and I found that I had to leave the beach at once. I sat in the car, reflecting on what had happened. I had no great enlightenment, but I felt it was some sort of spiritual experience. I had been on the same beach as the hundreds who had been there during the previous day, except with a different mindset. It is this mindset that enables reflection to take place. I can wander through a day, and never really hear or see anything. As Jesus said, 'They have eyes but they see not, they have ears but they hear not.'

As I sit on the park bench, or stroll around the pathways, I see life in its every form. I love to watch children in a park. They make full use of the space. They remind me when I go with friends to some place for a walk, and they bring the dog. As soon as the dog is let off the leash he just goes crazy. He races all over the place. He runs around in circles, he approaches other people, and he checks out every dog in sight. The impression I get from children is the sense of freedom they feel in a park. This must be some contrast to those who are confined to a high-rise apartment, or who live dangerously close to a busy motorway. It is uplifting to see the exuberance of these children. On the other hand, there is an elderly person sitting on a park bench, taking a rest after a short stroll. The contrast is quite striking, and I sometimes try to look out through that person's eyes to imagine what things must look like for them. Quite a lot of this is fairly superficial, of course, but when I am ready, I can move on to some serious reflection, and see where it brings me. The park can become a prayer room, if I so choose. The inner reflection, of course, is prompted and inspired by the Spirit of God within.

Spirit and breath of God, please give me a listening heart, a heart that hears the whispers that come to me, as I reflect on what I see around me. Help me to ponder these things in my heart, so as to be nourished and sustained. May my eyes be the windows of my soul, and may what I hear and see be the food of my spirit, as I reflect on the presence and action of God in the world around me.

Reflection is much more than just observing what is going on around me. It can result from something that comes into my mind in total isolation, completely detached from where I am, or what I see. It can be a recall of a childhood memory, or of something I heard or read. My reflection can lead to meditation. Reflection is the result of an idea arising in the mind, as a result of some verbal or mental comment. Meditation brings this a step further, in that it can be more structured or confined, involving a theme, a subject, or a passage. This can lead to contemplation which is sitting with a thought or an image, becoming part of it, as I gaze upon it, and hearing within the spirit whatever response that evokes. Reflection is the gateway to depth of soul, and to an inner richness of spirit that greatly nourishes our quality of life.

Living in a material world can make reflection quite difficult, and even make it appear as a waste of time. I can be seen as a dreamer. The artist is a dreamer, who sees things not seen by others. Happy are they who dream dreams, and are prepared to pay the price to make those dreams come true. Life can become very superficial, where we just skim the surface, and never really live. Everybody dies, but not everybody lives. Some people settle for existing. This is sad, because our lives can be greatly enriched when we avail of the mind, the imagination, and the soul to reflect on all that is happening, and become part of that, rather than being some sort of passive cabbage, devoid of all reaction. Jesus came that we should have life, and have it to the full. I think it only right that I should be held responsible for what I do with the wonderful gift of life. I only get one shot at it; there are no dress rehearsals. I have often heard it said that few people have died regretting that they didn't work more. They might well regret their compulsion to work, and their unavailability to smell the flowers. Being driven by the work ethic can turn us into robots, spiritless creatures, devoid of creativity, and every form of initiative. Reflection ensures that we plough a much wider and deeper score as we move through the field of life.

There are many books written on prayer, and there are as many ways of praying as there are people. I don't think there is one way better than another. One of the problems I had with prayer was that I tried to pray as others did. I saw those who could sit for long periods, completely motionless, with eyes closed. I tried to copy this, only to find that, after a few minutes, I'd be up and off, or my mind would begin wandering all over the place. I now find that reflection is very closely connected to prayer. It leads to a prayerful spirit. The Spirit of God speaks in the gentle breeze of whispers and, during reflection, it becomes possible to hear those whispers. It is a wonderful gift to have a prayerful spirit. This leads to inner peace, and produces a gentle spirit. As I said at the beginning of this chapter, a life without reflection is not worth living.

Tolerance

There is much talk today about racism and what is now called xenophobia, which is a morbid dislike of foreigners. For the first time, Ireland is being opened up to being a pluralist society, and the transition is not an easy one. A lot of intolerance stems from fear and ignorance, a fear that stems from not understanding, from being threatened, from blind bigotry. We continue to see this in the north of Ireland and, in recent years, we have the frightening prospects of a resurgence of the far right in France, Germany and England, where intolerance is spelt out in riots, violence, destruction, and death. Intolerance and bigotry is a frightening spectre, and I'm afraid we are going to see more of the same in the years ahead. The seat of such blind hatred is the human heart, and it is impossible to change this by legislation. This is uniquely the work of God's Spirit and, unfortunately, many of those to the forefront of this intolerance are not very open to any spirit that would counsel toleration, mutual respect, or live and let live.

The greatest obscenity of all, of course, is when this intolerance originates from some narrow-minded interpretation of the gospel message. We have killed many people in Jesus' name since the gospel was first entrusted to us. May the good Lord forgive us for such crimes against humanity, and against the message of love given us by Jesus.

Jesus' openness to others often got him into trouble, and contributed in no small way to his death. The society in which he lived was very intolerant. There were endless lists of people who were considered to be outside the pale.

They were inferior in every way, and religious Jews could have nothing to do with them. Jesus broke every convention of his race. He saw the person, and that person became the object of his interest, his pity, or his tolerance. This included public sinners, Samaritans, and Romans. All of this infuriated his enemies, but their fury did not deter his openness. He stood up to the religious leaders, and he condemned their bigotry and intolerance. This cost him dearly. He was quite explicit in his words and actions when it came to making contact with the 'outsiders'. He angered his listeners when he used the idea of a Samaritan as being more loving than a Jewish priest or Levite, in his story of the Good Samaritan. He defended the public sinner who washed his feet with her tears, and he held her up as being more loving than his host, the Pharisee. He touched the leper, something that was outrageous for anybody, especially a Jew. He healed the servant of the Roman officer, and he advocated that tax should be paid to Caesar, if that is what the law prescribed. A great deal of his teaching had to do with toleration, and acceptance of others. He even equated our treatment of others as treatment meted out to him personally. If I reject another because of colour, creed, nationality, or gender, Jesus takes that as rejecting him. Surely he couldn't possibly have laid greater emphasis on the importance of tolerance for all peoples.

There is a great blindness that goes with intolerance in any form. We all can hold our hands up and admit to our own form of intolerance. There are those who cannot tolerate children, and those who are very impatient with the elderly. A common topic of conversation among some elderly people is a criticism of the young, and how they do not conform to the strict moral code of behaviour, as practised in a former generation. I often joke that the only thing that is wrong with others is that they don't do things the way I do them! If they could only be like me, they would be perfect! The fact is that God decided, in his infinite wisdom, that one of me was enough, and so he made the others different. The blindness of which I speak can preclude any hope of actually seeing reality. It is a question of looking through tinted glasses. There is no way that such people can possibly see anything other than what they choose to see. The work of God's Spirit is to refocus their vision, and to enable them sing, 'I once was blind, but now I see.'

Spirit and breath of God, please remove all blindness from my heart and soul. Open my eyes to see the person, and not the colour of the skin, the human condition, or the other unimportant details on which we often place our bigoted judgements. Expand my heart, so that it may be open to all of God's people. Please help me to minister to others, believing that, in this way, I am ministering to Jesus.

When I receive a present at Christmas, I don't throw it in the bin because I don't like the wrapping it came in. I will unwrap the gift, and leave the wrapping to one side, as being part of the gift, but not essential to it. I can easily reject people because I don't like the wrapping, whether that be the colour of the skin, the accent, or their place of worship. It takes time to unwrap the gift, and to get to know the person, and being willing to give that time is central to my expression of tolerance. 'He's really very nice when you get to know him.' Taking time to get to know others, listen to their point of view, and understand their values and interests, goes a long way towards dispelling the clouds of ignorance that give rise to bigotry and intolerance. Some years ago, I was chaplain in a residential home for the elderly, and a very important part of my ministry was to 'waste time' with individuals, listening to their story, and entering into their lonely world. This can be real love, because the end product is not tangible, and because the story will probably be repeated tomorrow, it requires a sense of service that requires sincere tolerance and acceptance. Quite often, the people I find most difficult to tolerate are those within my own house. I am not talking of human failings here, things that would annoy anyone. I speak of the human condition of the depressed, the hypochondriac, the sick, and the dependent. My patience with such people is a real expression of my tolerance. This is never easy but, once again, I need to remind myself that Jesus takes such ministry as being done for him.

There are borderline cases where my tolerance may be conditioned. I can follow God's example when he loves the sinner, while condemning the sin. Christian tolerance doesn't mean that I am prepared to give a fool's pardon to everybody, irrespective of what their behaviour is like. I can absolutely refuse to be an enabler for the alcoholic, or to minimise the crime to the pedophile. I will have to correct the errant behaviour of the young, and to condemn injustice wherever it raises its ugly head. Toleration is a positive attitude, and not some whim of fancy. It provides clear guides to behaviour, and it facilitates healthy and wholesome living. In general, it is a good motto to 'Live and let live'. Everybody is on this earth with as much right as me, and they are entitled to their share of the oxygen, and to equal space. I do not own my country, or my neighbourhood. We have witnessed the atrocities of ethnic cleansing in recent years, where whole peoples were driven out of a region, because they were deemed to have no right to live there. The Jews were denied the right to exist in the Europe of the last war. Such crimes continue to be perpetrated, and the chorus of disapproval can be quite muted. This may stem from a sense of powerlessness to roll back such evil forces. I can do something, however, if only ensuring that people in my neck of the woods are treated fairly, and with justice, tolerance, and respect. I sometimes wonder what it must feel like to be approaching death, realising that I have refused to give some people the right to share this planet with me. We all have a conscience, whether we listen to it or not. When I was a child I had a dog that looked guilty whenever he did something wrong! Surely, in such a situation, most people would see the futility and wrong of their actions. When their blindness follows them to the grave, they are most to be pitied. In the final run-down, they are not going to take up any more space in the ground than any of the rest of us.

This story is told about Alexander the Great by the Greek writer Plutarch. One day Alexander came upon Diogenes, the ancient philosopher, and he was examining some bones. He had two sets of bones in two different boxes. When Alexander asked him what he was doing, he said he was reflecting on some of the more important lessons of life. 'For example,' says Diogenes, 'the two sets of bones here are those of your father, and one of his slaves. I have examined them now for some time, and I honestly must confess that I cannot find any difference be-tween them!' 'Nuff said!

Simplicity

I believe that simplicity is a wonderful virtue, but it may not be seen as such. There can be a vast difference between being intellectual and being intelligent. The intellectual tends to complicate things with definitions, and a vocabulary that is outside the usage of the ordinary punter. Simplicity is to keep things simple, to avoid complications, and to be clear and definite in what I wish to say. 'Keep it simple' is an excellent motto, that is part of the Alcoholics Anonymous programme of recovery. It is reckoned that the simpler and the less complicated the programme is, the more likely it is that people will follow it.

There are people who are very complicated. They are unable to call a spade a spade, when they can refer to it as an agricultural implement. The language of bureaucracy, and the language of the legal eagles is notoriously complicated. It is only in recent years that forms coming in the front door of homes, to be completed and returned, are written in language that is capable of being understood. I understand that legal language often has to be precise, concise, and very much in legal terminology. A wrong word here or there could open up the way for a different interpretation. When I speak of simplicity in this chapter, I speak more of a way of life, than a way of speaking. I will, however, continue to speak of simple ways of communication for a while.

I wrote a book some years ago that is still available on the shelves. It is called *It's Really Very Simple*, and is subtitled *Uncomplicating the message*. I wrote that book because I often feel that some people give up on trying to understand what the homilist is saying, or what the Pope or bishop are getting at in that last letter. I dedicated the book to a little old lady I met as I came out of a church one night, after preaching at a Novena. She caught me by the arm, and she whispered, 'God bless you, Father. I'm going to say a prayer for you, because even I understood what you were saying!' I often thought of her, and I know there are many more like her out there.

Jesus was very simple in his method of teaching. Being a brilliant teacher, he brought his listeners from the known to the unknown. He spoke of fish, birds, vines, and trees, things that were visible to his listeners even as he spoke. His secret was to begin where they were, to speak to them where they were at. He spoke about very abstract concepts like the kingdom of heaven, or the final judgement, and he did so by referring to sorting out the catch of fish in a net, or about the reward awaiting the giving of a cup of water. Our human gifts were spoken of as coins entrusted to us for investment, and our lack of faith was compared to the freedom of the birds of the air. He spoke of his message being so simple that the intellectual and the worldly wise would never comprehend it. We have to become uncomplicated, and have the heart of a child, if we wish to enter the kingdom of God.

The faith of many who were healed in the gospel is particularly extraordinary, because many of them were simple, unlettered, and unreligious folk. The little woman in the crowd, who touched the hem of his garment, is someone who always gets my respect. She had no airs and graces. She had a physical ailment, and she had not got better, despite spending every penny she had over twelve years. Her situation was simple. She had nowhere to go, and she turned to Jesus, without any great or impressive prayer. I do not understand the source of her faith, except to say that her failure up till now had narrowed her options, and her openness to the goodness that she saw in

Jesus, inspired her to throw discretion to the wind, and to go for it. There was no long-winded speech of petition. 'If I touch the hem of his garment, I will be healed.' It was as simple as that. This scene is repeated many times in the gospel. 'Lord, that I may see ... Lord, if you will, you can make me clean ... Jesus, Son of David, have mercy on me.' This simple faith is extraordinary, and I can only think of one explanation for it. The presence of Jesus, and the sense of love and goodness that he exuded, awoke a sense of trust in them, gave them hope, and generated a cry from their hearts. Without they themselves knowing it, it had to be the Spirit of God within, whether that person was a Roman, a Samaritan, or a Jew. God has no grandchildren. We are all children of God, irrespective of race, creed, or colour.

On several occasions, we read where someone attempted to engage Jesus in a debate. This was the case with the woman at the well, the argument over taxes, the questions about divorce or remarriage, or whether he should heal on the Sabbath or not. Jesus was not one who lived up in his head, and he refused to be drawn into debate. He took their line of argument, turned it around, and tossed the question back to them. He saw that they were being deliberately obstructive, and were not prepared to deviate from their stubbornness. We are told that, on one occasion, he was annoyed at their hardness of heart, and he refused to enter into debate with them. People who insist on complicating something that is essentially simple can be very aggravating and, indeed, very devious. I believe that I can be too intellectual to grasp the message of the gospel, but I cannot be too stupid. For those who don't understand, no words are possible, and for those who do understand, no words are necessary.

The lifestyle of Jesus was very simple. He wandered around from place to place, sleeping wherever or whenever he got a chance. His lifestyle does not have a great practical interest for us, because of its nomadic nature, and because lifestyle in general in those days would surely have been fairly simple, if not even very basic. I do, however, believe that his priorities were fairly uncomplicated. He had a single-minded approach to everything, including life. He was here with a mission, 'and how can I be at peace until it is completed,' as he himself said. His life was simple in that he never lost sight of his mission and, because he never compromised the truth, he never had to untangle himself from any of life's meshes. His fundamental option never varied, he did not swing with the popular flow, nor was he engaged in some sort of sell techniques that would have caused him to tailor his message to the tastes of his listeners. His life was simple in that there was a consistent thread running right through it. He stuck to the truth and, unlike election manifestos, his eight Beatitudes were principles that would remain firm, and his word was something that we could count on. 'Heaven and earth will pass away before my word passes away.'

I believe that God is infinitely simple. I don't fully understand what that means, and I accept that, even in eternity, I may still not fully comprehend the fullness of that. Thomas Aquinas says that whatever we say about God, there is only one thing we can be sure of, and that is that we are wrong. God is more than anything I could say about him. I could not think of God as being complicated, even if I fail to comprehend infinite simplicity. St John tells us that God is love. John's gospel is the one that is most theological, and laden with imagery and grand statements. There is contrast between life and death, darkness and light, good and evil. He speaks of Jesus as the Word, and of that Word becoming flesh. Later in life, as an old man in exile on the island of Pathmos, he has reduced the message to one simple mantra: 'God is love ... We ought to love one another, because God has loved us ... In this is love, not that we love God, but that God first loved us ... If you live in love, God lives in you, and you live in God ... Little children, let us love one another.' He has reduced all the theological concepts to the simple refrain of loving God, and loving one another. That is about as simple as we could ask for.

There is something very attractive about simple, uncomplicated people. There is a genuineness about them, because they are devoid of duplicity and deviousness. They are reliable and trustworthy. They don't operate with a hidden agenda, and we can trust them, and their word. They are wonderful and faithful friends and, because their lives are uncomplicated, they appear to be thoughtful and kind. Goodness is a way of life with them, and they are very rich people, even if they are not wealthy. Richness has nothing to do with money. They are rich in personality, and in a generous heart. They are children in the best sense of that word, who still retain a sense of wonder, an ability to be grateful, and the freedom to enjoy. The Spirit must surely be their life-blood, even if they are not aware of it. There is a transparency about them that could only come from the Spirit of God living within. It is difficult to disguise the presence of the Spirit, and simplicity is one of the ways in which the inner Spirit reveals his presence.

Spirit and breath of God, please create a spirit of simplicity within my heart. Rid me of all deviousness and duplicity. Help me to be genuine in my dealings with others, so that my 'yes' is 'yes'. Please give me a spirit of gentleness that is not complicated by manipulation and double-think. May your presence within me shine out to all I meet, through the words I say, and the things I do.

Action

One of the ways of doing nothing is to think about it, or talk about it, long enough. Quite often, when all is said and done, there's much more said than done! There is no scarcity of ideas, but there's nothing more powerful than an idea whose time has come.

The gospel is about action, and the questions that Jesus tells us which will make up the General Judgement, are scandalously materialistic, in that they are about feeding the hungry, giving a drink to the thirsty, clothing the naked, visiting the prisoner, and welcoming the stranger. The story of the ten virgins tells of those who didn't get around to doing something until it was too late. They knew it had to be done, but they decided that should be at some other time. Jesus came 'to do and to teach'. He came to do firstly, and only then would he point to this as a lesson on how we ought to act. The gospel is not just something to believe or accept, it is a plan of action.

You write a new page of the gospel each day,
by the things that you do, and the words that you say.
People read what you write, whether faithful or true.
What is the gospel according to you?

If you want to get something done, ask a busy person. The others are so busy thinking of all they have to do, that they are actually doing nothing. I remember a student who was highly critical of a teacher, because he had watched the teacher spend nearly an hour trying to get a close-up photograph of a bee's wings in action. The student was quite scathing about such a waste of time, while being totally oblivious of the fact that he himself had just spent one

hour watching the other, and actually doing nothing! At
least the teacher was pursuing a goal, and was fully intent
on seeing it through.

The person with the healthy disposition is someone
who acts immediately, and who does today what should
be done today. This is the sign of an organised mind, when
the idea or the decision is translated into action. Many
ideas and decisions are still-born, and never come to
fruition. The message of Christmas is 'peace on earth to
those of goodwill'. This goodwill, of course, must be put
into action, or else it remains as a good idea. I have often
looked at an untidy office, or a bedroom with more items
of clothes draped across chairs than hanging up in a
wardrobe, and I thought that I should tackle this some-
time. The person of action would have done the job when I
was deciding that I would get around to it. We are all familiar with the wise men, sitting on high stools in pubs,
holding forth on the evils of the world, and what the government or the local authorities should do to put things
right. There is no end to their theories, but they are very
short on action. The fact is that the country will not be any
better off the following morning. In fact, within their
throbbing heads, it may be much worse! So much for
bright ideas!

I said earlier that there was nothing more powerful
than an idea whose time had come. Some of the greatest
movements for good in the history of the world were
brought about by people who were people of action; who
got an idea, and acted on it; who saw what needed to be
done, and did it. Such people are real sources of blessing
for all of us, and thank God for them. They are trail-blaz-
ers, even if they go about their work in a quiet, discreet
way. They let their actions speak, and these are more powerful than any words. 'What you do speaks so loudly, that I
cannot hear what you're saying.' They lead by example,
and they are a wonderful influence wherever they are. We

see this in every area of life. There are those who join com-
mittees, and who are to the front in organising anything
that is for the local, or the common good. They organise a
neighbourhood, and set up a neighbourhood watch. They
run clubs and football teams for the young. They mobilise
local talent, and set up competitions, sports, and venture
endeavours. While they could be at home, with their feet
up, they are out there, running all over the place, getting
an area to waken up to its responsibilities, motivating people to be part of a solution rather than remain as part of a
problem. They are a leaven in the community, and they are
very life-giving people.

Jesus was a person of action. When Jairus asked for
help, he said he would go with him straightaway. He said
the same to the centurion, who objected, claiming that he
was not worthy to have Jesus under his roof. Jesus had
pity on the crowds and he decided to feed them, even
though he had nothing with which to do so. He would call
on the Father, because the situation was urgent and it
could not be put off. At another time, he felt sorry for the
crowds he saw, because they were like sheep without a
shepherd and, even though he was tired, he began to teach
them, knowing they had followed him to hear his words.
He was resolute in his determination to go to Jerusalem,
even though this would mean going to his death. Even
when Peter tried to persuade him to reconsider this, he
saw this as a temptation from Satan. Satan can be very
threatened by action, but is not at all concerned about nice
ideas and good intentions that lead to nothing. His call to
the apostles is a call to action. He sent them out with particular instructions as to what they were to do. They were
to be people with a mission and, as he said about his own
mission, 'How can I be at peace until it is accomplished?'
As he was dying on the cross he told the Father that he had
finished the task entrusted to him. Earlier he said that they
must be busy while they had time, because the time would

come when it would be difficult to work. The time will come for all of us when we will be confined to bed, or a wheelchair, and the days of activity will be over. In the meantime, however, like Jesus, we must be about our Father's business.

People of action are special people. If they promise to do something, you can depend on them doing it. There are others who are full of good intentions, but if you need something done soon, it is much safer to do it yourself. People of action make good and reliable friends. It's extraordinary to watch ambitious people, and those who are in the fast lane, where making money is their primary concern. They are compulsive goers, and seem prepared to keep going till they drop. Indeed, some of them do drop with a heart attack, as early as forty years of age. They are people of action with a vengeance, but their motives are selfish. It is quite significant to see how energetic we can get when there is a reward at the end of the line. The kind of people I am interested in are those who go into action because something needs to get done, and most of this is in the line of duty, part of home life, or a favour for someone else. They are the hewers of wood and the drawers of water. They are the basin and towel people who, like Jesus in the gospel, always seem to be at the service of others.

In his novel *The Fall*, Albert Camus tells of a solicitor who is in a red light district in Amsterdam. He hears a woman scream, and he suspects that she has been thrown into the canal. He dismisses his instinct to help, because he doesn't want to become involved. Supposing there are cameras there, and he is seen in such an area. Maybe if he went to help, he, too, would be attacked by whoever attacked her. He is debating thus in his mind, when her screams die down, and he knows now that it is too late. Camus finishes his description with a chilling comment: 'He didn't do anything, because that was the kind of person he was.' What a comment! I have heard put-downs, but that is one that no one would like. To be a person who just doesn't do anything … What a purposeless life! It is hardly right to think of such a person as being alive at all. On the Day of Judgment, Jesus speaks of those who will be condemned as those who had the opportunities to do the good, but who squandered or neglected them. Like the priest and the levite passing by the man lying on the road to Jericho. They didn't hurt him, spit on him, or call him names. They simply passed by and did nothing. My life will be judged as much on what I didn't do as by what I did.

The people of action are alive and alert, and they avail of the opportunities to act. Procrastination is the thief of time. Nothing gets done when it is going to get done some other time. The only time available to me is now. Jesus speaks of watching and praying. Unless I am alert, I won't see the opportunities for action. When the going gets tough, the tough get going. Some people have the rare gift of swinging into action without any great deliberation, because the task to be done needs action rather than consideration. Seeing a blind man standing at a pedestrian crossing doesn't require any profound reflection on our part. Most times it is obvious what needs to be done. The action is the outcome of an inner disposition. When I am disposed to be a helping person, I am ready for action once the opportunity arises. The promptings to action can so often be the action of God's Spirit within.

Spirit and breath of God please generate in me a willingness to be of help to others. Prompt me into action when the opportunity arises. Help me be alert, with an open heart to those in need, and to what needs to get done around me. Please help me anticipate the needs of others, when I can. Give me the love that shows itself in action.

Thoughtfulness

Thoughtfulness is the result of wearing rabbit's ears antennae on your head, so that you are always capable of picking up the vibes of what's going on around you, and are able to act. It involves a sensitivity to others, where the welfare of the other is a high priority. It is the external actions of someone with a good heart, who is not wrapped up in self, and who is available to others. Thoughtful people provide those special moments that make life worthwhile. They seem to have constant thought of others, and they seldom have to be asked to help. A thoughtful spouse, child, or friend is a wonderful gift, because they are always in the business of making others feel worthwhile. They are there when we need them, and they are generally low-key, and quiet when they act. It seems to be like a second nature with them, as their actions appear to be so spontaneous, and just exactly the right thing to do. They don't parade their goodness, but those of us who benefit from their goodness cannot fail to notice, and to be impressed.

We live in a world where the increasing pressures of life tend to cause people to be busy and preoccupied with something or other. The great stress is on material things, and the compulsion is to acquire and accumulate. It is so easy to get caught up in this rat-race. It is easy to become so busy with the urgent that I overlook the important. The pursuit of false gods can make achievers of us all. Life can become a performance marathon, and there may be no time for the things that really matter. Time becomes very precious when it can bring a high rate of earnings by the hour. With the escalating price of houses, cars, etc., some people avail of every hour they can get in the workplace. It is easy to see how one's world can become narrowed down until very few people inhabit it. While I understand all of the above, I am grateful that we have others who would never sell their soul for anything. Life is too precious for them, and the greatest riches they have in life are people. They treasure others, they see themselves connected to others, and they cannot imagine a life apart from others. Some people have a heart as big as the great outdoors, and they are always making space in their hearts for others. They include others in many of their decisions, and they are always eager to share a new discovery, some useful idea, or an adventure that comes on the horizon. They inspire and enthuse others because they have an openness to others that make this possible. They are a leaven among their families and friends. Their thoughtfulness inspires others to do likewise, and they generate gratitude within the heart of others. It is not possible to be grateful and unhappy at the same time, so the gratitude they inspire also evokes happiness within the hearts of the recipients of their goodness.

It goes without saying that Jesus was thoughtful. He sent the apostles away for a rest while he dismissed the crowd. One of the apostles suggested that he send the people home because they were hungry, but he suggested that they themselves should feed them. After his resurrection, when the apostles had spent the night without catching any fish, he told them where to play out the nets. When the boat was full of fish, and they got to shore, he was waiting on them, with a fire lit, ready to cook some of the fish for their breakfast. Even as he died on the cross he entrusted his mother to the care of his friend John, and he asked his mother to take care of John. He turned to one of the men being put to death with him and he promised him heaven that very day. His washing the feet of his apostles was

hardly a once-off of such humble service because, with a
heart like his, he must surely have given many a touching
display of thoughtfulness and love. He said that his heart
was meek and humble, and being thoughtful is surely the
action of someone with such a heart. There is a gentleness
and humility about those who are thoughtful about the
welfare of others. They have an ordered priority that
guides them in their actions, where the #1 is God, #2 is
others, and #3 is self. Sin consists in changing those num-
bers around in any way. If I act in such a way that I succeed
in keeping myself last, then I must surely be a very
thoughtful person.

In this book so far, I have written on Service, Compassion, and Action. Thoughtfulness would be part of any
of those. I chose to give it a special chapter, however, because I consider it to be important enough to warrant this.
A thoughtful person is unique, and to be a thoughtful person is a wonderful blessing. Any one of us can cultivate
this attitude and, if we do, we are destined to become
sources of blessing for others, and the recipients of many
blessings ourselves. We become blessed in the giving, and
we join that unique group that I would designate as The
Happiest People in the World. In Dickens' story, *The
Christmas Carol*, when Scrooge kept everything for himself,
he continued to be grumpy and miserable. It was only
when he began to give to others that he entered into the
spirit of Christmas, and he was completely transformed.
Thoughtful people contribute through their happiness as
much as through their actions.

I would consider being thoughtful as being one of the
qualities of the mature Christian. Thoughtfulness comes
from being alert to what's going on around me, and being
ready to respond to what happens. Jesus told us to 'Watch
and pray'. Pray, by all means, but be alert as well, or the
moments of grace will pass you by. There are endless opportunities for doing good presented in the course of each

day. Only those who are in touch with the inner Spirit will be alert enough to be aware of these, and be willing enough to respond to them.

Spirit and breath of God, I ask you, please, to give me a keen sense of awareness of others, and of their needs. I depend on you to alert me to what is happening around me, and to inspire me with a gift of gentle caring to minister in what way I can to those who need my help. Please make me an angel of mercy who is genuinely concerned for the good of others.

The thoughtful person is like a paramedic who is never sure when a need may arise. It is not some sort of crusade. Rather is it a quiet, caring presence. I go about my own work, with full attention to that work. The opportunity to do a good turn for another may not arise and, if it does, I may not be free to do anything about it. The person may need a lift somewhere, and I am at work and I may not leave. I'm not in the business of helping others at the expense of duty, responsibility, or some more urgent need. All of my helping must be tempered with common sense and prudence.

The greatest blessing provided by the really thoughtful person is witnessed at home. It is easy to be a street angel and a house devil. The most difficult place to practise the gospel is in my own kitchen. When I look at the injustices in the world today, I could easily throw up my hands in despair. I wouldn't know where to begin. A useful rule-of-thumb is to stay at home and to start at home. I remember a pupil in school being quite dismissive of efforts at world peace. 'Don't talk to me about world peace. We can't have a moment's peace in our own house.' Most of us are involved in two communities. We live in one and with one, and we go out the door each morning into the other. What happens in that first community is brought out the door as we head to work. I can be burdened with a lot of baggage as I go out the door in the morning. The people I meet that day will certainly suffer because of that. If, however, I am a thoughtful person, who practises thoughtfulness within my own kitchen, then I become a blessing to others as I head out to meet the day. One community is benefiting greatly by the other. My actions during the day in the workplace can generate more goodwill and openness to others, and my home community benefits greatly each time I return.

I remember it said about a person that it wasn't so much that she suffered from depression, but that she was a carrier! The opposite is true for the person with a kind heart. They spread goodness wherever they go. I don't believe we can renew people, nor can we corrupt people. We renew the atmosphere in which they live, and they become renewed, or we corrupt the atmosphere in which they work, and they become corrupted. I have a much better chance of nurturing Christian living in a parish if I can develop a Christian atmosphere within that parish. We take on causes on behalf of the oppressed, and we develop programmes on behalf of the marginalised. The lives of the people involved in these programmes will change as a result, as they become more aware of others and of their needs. Naturally, there are people who would never be part of such endeavours, and the only thing to do is to leave them to it, and to get on with what's in hand. If Jesus waited for everybody to listen to him, he would not have started yet. 'If each before his own door swept, the whole village would be clean.' All any of us can do is to do the best with what we have.

Thoughtfulness is such an intrinsic virtue that I either have it or I don't. However, I believe that it is something I can develop, even if my attempts are more laboured, and not as free-flowing as the one with a natural gift of thoughtfulness. The Spirit must surely play a role here, and I believe that if I declare my willingness to be available here, that the practice will become second nature for me. It is better to light a candle than curse the darkness.

A thoughtful person is a real leaven in the community. The community is greatly enriched by each and every individual that travels this road. If what I have written awakens a desire within the heart of any individual to focus more on being thoughtful in their dealings with others, then this chapter will not be in vain. 'If I can help somebody as I pass along; if I can cheer somebody with a smile or song; if I can show somebody that he's travelling wrong, then my living will not be in vain.'

Speech

'A person who commits no offence in speech is perfect, and capable of ruling the whole self. We put a bit into a horse's mouth to master it and with this we control its whole body. The same is true of ships; however big they are, and driven by strong winds, the helmsman steers them with a tiny rudder. In the same way, the tongue is a tiny part of the body, but it is capable of great things.' This is what St James had to say all those many years ago. His words are just as true today. Notice that he says 'great things'. He goes on to mention that, like a tiny flame which sets fire to a whole building, the tongue is capable of much harm. For the purposes of this reflection, I hope to concentrate on the good that can be effected by responsible use of speech.

Speech is an extraordinary gift, and it is something we can easily take for granted. For most people, it is their primary means of communication and, only when we come across people communicating in signs, do we become aware of other means of everyday communication. It is quite significant that people are dumb, not because they cannot speak, but because they cannot hear. Children learn to speak by imitating the sounds they hear. If they are deaf, they cannot hear those sounds and, therefore, they will not be able to speak. Speech that is connected to hearing tends to be more meaningful, because it is a response to what is heard. I have two ears and one mouth, so I should listen twice as much as I speak!

Speech can sometimes be the weakest form of communication. When I am in the presence of tragedy, or of great sorrow, it is often better not to speak, but to reach out a hand, to share a tear, to embrace the suffering one. Attempts to speak at such times are often insensitive, and unhelpful. 'For those who understand, no words are necessary.' My actions often speak louder than my words, and there are times when it is better that this is so. It is sometimes impossible to put a deep feeling into words, and it is generally advisable not to try.

Jesus made full use of his gift of speech. He must have had a strong voice, to be heard above the heads of vast throngs, in those days before we had amplification. He preached on the mountain-side, from a boat, or in the Temple. He must have had a voice that commanded attention, and this would have come from the conviction that goes with something being said that is true. He proclaimed his message, rather than spoke it. When I speak from the heart, I speak to the heart. He must have had a voice that got immediate attention. It was obvious the people understood what he was saying, because they hung on his words, and they followed him for days to listen to him.

Words, of themselves, mean nothing. I meet one person who asks me how I am, and I don't tell him, because it is obvious from the tone of voice that the person doesn't want to know. I meet someone else who asks me the same question, and I tell him, often to such an extent that he's sorry he asked me! It is never the words; it is the spirit in the words that matters. I remember something from many years ago, when I was a teacher. I took over from another teacher, and I discovered that the class was very upset with that person. When I asked what had caused the upset, I was told that she had delivered a blistering scolding in which she told them they were uncooperative, noisy, and ungrateful. As it happened, I got on well with this class, and they knew that I liked them and never minded coming in to them. I sat down on the front desk, and I showed them how uncooperative, noisy, and ungrateful they really were! They listened to me, and had no problem with what I said, because my words were not sharp, nor was my attitude strident. The same words, delivered with a very different spirit. It is here that Jesus would have been most effective. His love must surely have come through in what he said. Certainly, there was no disguising his sincerity.

Jesus combined his words with action. He expressed his sympathy for the hungry crowds, and he fed them. He spoke of having the heart of a child, as he hugged the children. His actions never contradicted his words. He was always consistent in what he said, because the facts are friendly, and when I speak the truth I never have to change my story. There was something about his tone of voice that engendered confidence in others to dare approach him. It is unlikely that the little woman in the crowd ever met him before, but she probably heard him. That was enough to convince her that he was someone who could be approached, and she would not suffer rejection. His were words that touched the spirit of his listeners. They were words that came from a heart on fire with love, and with a sense of mission, and of urgency for something that needed to be accomplished. He used his gift of speech as a means of teaching, of healing, of correcting, and of commanding. The devils recoiled before his words. His words were like two-edged swords that penetrated the hearts of his listeners and called on them for a response. The great advantage that I have as a Christian, is that I can have the same Spirit in my words as I speak.

Spirit and breath of God, please anoint and empower my words. Please be in every word I speak, so that my words may help, heal, and enlighten. Give life to my words that they may inspire and console. Anoint me with the gift of prophecy, that I might speak God's word to those I meet.

The gift of speech is a very real way of building up God's kingdom. I can make my speech available to the Spirit, who anoints my words, and gives them a power and a force that I never could. It is sad to think of the many wasted words that float around in the atmosphere, going nowhere, doing nothing. The Spirit of God can do wonders with our words, when we make our gift of speech available for his work. We become channels of peace, of healing, of comfort, and of consolation. It would be wonderful to develop the habit of whispering a short prayer to the Spirit before I make a phone call, enter a home, share at a meeting, or write a letter. My words may not change, but they will be blessed, and they will contain a power which I could never give them. 'When you stand to speak on my behalf,' says Jesus, 'don't worry what you shall say, because the Spirit will give you words that your enemies will not be able to contradict.' It is wonderful to have access to such power, and it is a great privilege to be able to promote God's kingdom by such a simple gift as speech.

It is very difficult to undo the harm done by words. It is like scattering a sack of feathers, and then setting out to collect them after they have been blown all over the place by the wind. If I'm not responsible in my use of speech when I share something that was confidential, or tell of something without having the facts, I have set in motion a whole whirlwind that wrecks havoc wherever it goes. The words pass from one person to another and it is impossible to head it off. I believe it is only right that I should be held responsible for my use of my gift of speech. It is too precious a gift to be entrusted without requiring accountability. While it can be such a powerful force for good, it can also contribute to much harm and destruction.

We sometimes speak of people who seem to have no connection between their brains and their tongue. They just throw out rumour as fact, and they even make pronouncements on issues which are away beyond their knowledge. Such people are dangerous, and their speech can be very destructive. Listening to such people serves to confirm them, so it is also dangerous to provide them with an audience. There are times when I just have to refuse to listen any more, either by saying so or by excusing myself to attend some other engagement. Bringing my listening to such an abrupt end may appear discourteous, but I don't think I have any choice. Usually it is futile to engage such people in a discussion about the accuracy of their reports. I may, of course, make a point about not believing what is being said. In the final analysis, however, it is much better to get out of that situation.

It is a special grace to take responsibility for my gift of speech. It is a wonderful gift, and can be the means of many blessings for those I meet. The tongue, as St James says, is very difficult to control. When I consecrate that gift to the Lord, and accept it as a special ingredient in my Christian living, I will always be alert in my use of it, and I will never take it for granted. Just as I use my tongue to pray, so I can use it in my relationships with others. I will try to be faithful to the truth, and let my 'yes' be 'yes', and my 'no' be 'no'. I will use it to confirm others, as well as thank them, apologise to them and, where appropriate, to correct them. I will avoid flattery and empty and idle words. I will avail of the Communion resting on my tongue as a moment when I can rededicate this gift to God's glory, and to the good of those I meet. God has given me this gift for others. He didn't give me my gift of speech to go around talking to myself!

Acceptance

Acceptance is about living in reality. It is about seeing things as they are, and recognising that this is so. It involves what is capable of being done, and what is impossible. 'Lord, give me the serenity to accept the things I cannot change ...' There is freedom in accepting the things I cannot change, because it frees me from holding on to a pipe-dream. I cannot change yesterday, nor can I change another human being. By accepting reality, it prevents me wasting time trying to do the impossible. There is a journey that brings me to acceptance. I have a friend who is a recovering alcoholic. I saw how long it took him to admit that he was an alcoholic. He went to AA meetings, but was unable to say 'I am an alcoholic.' It was as if saying it would make him one! It took quite a further length of time before he was able to believe that he was an alcoholic. It was yet some time later before he actually accepted the truth of his alcoholism. Eventually, he even came to understand that fact, and the exact ramifications for him, as a result of that fact. Probably the acceptance was the most difficult, and he fought it all the way. He was determined to prove that he could stay away from alcohol, and prove to everyone, including himself, that he was not an alcoholic. Sometimes the truth hurts, but it also frees us from a bondage that controls our lives. Acceptance can open the door to freedom.

Acceptance is a word that covers many issues. Acceptance of others can be a real form of non-judging love. Jesus had an extraordinary acceptance for sinners, for the broken and the marginalised. Love is to accept someone exactly as that person is. Jesus had great compassion for the leper, the blind, the lame. He could see the innocence behind the outward appearance. Not only did he accept the appearance of the leper, but he reached out to the person himself, and made him feel accepted. This ability to see beyond the outward guise, enabled him to see the hypocrisy of the Pharisees, or the deviousness of the Scribe. This he would not accept, because to do so would be giving approval and acceptance to something he abhorred. His acceptance was certain for those of goodwill, and of a good heart, no matter how ugly, repulsive, or offputting the outer appearance might be. He accepted the public sinner, while telling her to sin no more. This was not a condemnation, but more of a word of advice about something that had nearly cost her her life.

Acceptance has truth as its core. The Christian must never accept a situation that involves injustice. Neither should a Christian accept behaviour that is immoral, or destructive of human relationships. Acceptance is never about giving approval to something that is obviously wrong. It is a very positive virtue, and it is never about giving a fool's pardon just for the sake of being popular. As a Christian, there are situations in which I do not belong, and there is conduct which I cannot accept. It is important that I exercise my moral courage in taking decisions and acting appropriately, when this is called for. I can be complicit in the wrong when, through moral cowardice or for some selfish motive, I go along with something which is against my Christian ethic. Acceptance involves judgement in certain situations, although this may be quite infrequent.

'I was wrong' is a much more honest confession than to say 'I did wrong.' The first statement stands on its own, and does not need to be qualified. The second can allow for several conditions or qualifications. 'I did wrong, but it was your fault ... I forgot ... I was conned into it ... the

devil made me do it.' 'I was wrong' involves total acceptance of my role in the incident or event. It is acceptance
without waffling, or malingering. I accept my responsibility
without excuse. There would never be a war of any kind if
someone, somewhere, was willing to say 'I was wrong'.
Because of the unwillingness of someone to accept responsibility, millions of innocent people may lose their lives. It
is frightening when we have people who refuse to accept
responsibility for their actions. It often appears that many
of these just don't seem capable of doing so. It is important, however, that I bring this concept nearer home, and
examine my own track record in this matter. Let there be
justice in the world, and let it begin with me. To hope to
change the world means staying at home and starting at
home.

I believe that acceptance can play a very important part
in one's own state of happiness. There are people who
have never accepted the conditions in which they were
reared. They feel hard-done-by in their person, relative to
appearance, ability, or talents. They feel inferior to others,
and they are convinced that life has dealt them a lousy
hand. God can come in for some of the blame, and he often
does. There is a whole journey towards acceptance that
must be undertaken here. This is usually best done with a
counsellor or a therapist. Usually the person's opinion of
self is quite erroneous, but even if it's not, there is no other
option available but acceptance. We all have our own gifts,
and everyone of us is good at something. There are areas
of life where improvement can be made, because none of
us is beyond redemption. There was a very popular movie
some years ago called *The Elephant Man*, that was based on
a true story. Someone came across a man who had been in-
stitutionalised because of his grotesque appearance. He
was called the Elephant Man, because his facial expression
looked more like that of an elephant than a human. The
person who discovered him, found that he was highly in-

telligent, extremely gentle and loving and, behind the appearance, was a really beautiful human being. It is possible that the man is still alive, and he is now a world celebrity; not in a voyeuristic way, where people would go along to gawk at him, but where people go to him to listen to his words of wisdom, and to learn his philosophy of life that enables him feel whole, despite such obvious obstacles. The story of the movie is about acceptance; how the man became to be accepted, and how he had learned to accept his situation.

From a practical point of view, I think of acceptance as having to do with a dimension of loving. In an earlier reflection on Tolerance, I spoke of racism, bigotry, and xenophobia. This behaviour stems from ignorance, and an inability to see and to accept. To be an accepting person is to be a generous person – someone whose love can reach out to others, irrespective of their human condition, ability, or human endowment. It betokens an open heart, where the other finds a welcome. I believe that the root of this virtue is found in my acceptance of myself, and situations in my own life. To accept myself, exactly as I am, is not as common as we would hope for. Some people just cannot, or refuse to see any good in themselves. It is difficult, if not impossible, for such people to see the good in others. They either reject this good, or they are jealous of it. Accepting myself involves many things. It includes accepting my age, the gifts I possess and exercise, the affirmation I receive from others, as well as my general appearance, and the level of comfort I enjoy in life. Acceptance of self leads to an inner balance that produces peace, and a sense of well-being. It produces inner health, and it gives me an anchor in life. I don't feel that I need apologise for my existence, nor am I beholden to others to make me feel good. Any affirmation from others is a bonus, but it is not necessary for my happiness. I can accept the mistakes I made in life, learn from them, and accept that I cannot change them, or make it that they never happened. Acceptance is like an undergirding support in my life, that keeps it even and balanced. I find that I like living in reality, and I have no desire to retreat to some sort of cloud-cuck-oo-land. My life becomes much more predictable, because the facts are friendly, and I find that I have a real desire to live in the truth. The truth always works.

Spirit and breath of God, please give me the serenity to accept the things I cannot change. Anoint my heart with a compassion that will enable me accept others as they are. Give me a constant sense of gratitude for what I have, and who I am. Please ensure that my feet are firmly planted in the soil of reality.

Change

'To live is to change, and to become perfect is to have changed often,' said Cardinal Newman. Life is about change, and nothing remains the same. There is not a cell in my body that was there seven years ago. Everything around us is in the process of change. We are growing older, the roads and buildings are getting more worn, and the trees are getting taller. It must be very difficult living in this world of rapid change, if I cannot accept change. With the explosion of communications, technology, and world travel, change is happening at an ever-increasing rate. And yet there are people bemoaning the past, who wish to remain in some sort of time-warp where everything remains the same. They are continually giving out about everything in today's world and, while having to live in that world, they must be constantly unhappy. This does not always follow an age pattern, because some elderly people get excited with change, while younger folks can feel very threatened by it.

I think that fear is at the core of their unhappiness. They are afraid of change, because they feel they are being left behind. They continually go on about being completely ignorant when it comes to television, VCR's, computers, mobile phones, etc. Instead of making an effort to familiarise themselves with any of these conveniences, they have decided that they were better off before these things came on the scene, and they dismiss them as being an intrusion. The story is told about an old lady who got a television, and she was totally convinced that there was much better weather when she only had a wireless! Now there are lows coming in from the Atlantic, and the winds are all blowing at different strengths, and there is a different number for the temperature all over the country.

Change is what gives variety to life. It only begins to effect me for good, when I myself begin to change. Life is a dynamic, it is always changing and evolving. It is never static. There is no such thing as standing still. If I am not changing for the better, I am changing for the worse. If I am not moving forward, I can be sure that I'm moving backwards. I must be involved in the process of change, or I'm dead. Alice in Wonderland says in the first sentence of that book, 'I could tell you my story beginning this morning. I couldn't begin yesterday, because I was a different person then.' While there have always been strong arguments for and against evolution, there can be no gainsaying the fact of there being constant evolution in our everyday lives. If you ever waken up some morning and you discover that your life is exactly the way it should be, don't move; just stay there, and wait for the undertaker! You have died during the night, and the process of change is over. You are now all that God created you to be. This side of the grave involves constant change 'until Christ be formed in us,' as St Paul says.

Jesus was to the forefront with enormous change. He encountered those who saw the law literally carved in stone, which did not allow for change of any kind. He was continually challenging the status quo. 'The law says to you … but I say to you …' 'A new commandment I give to you …' The religious leaders were not prepared to change and, rather than do so, they had to get rid of him. Religious people have a real problem with change. Some people have never accepted the Mass in the vernacular, and still frequent a Latin Mass wherever it is available. They see religion as being immutable, as something that always was and ever shall be. They are trapped in the past, and are totally unwilling to let go of that. There are a few things that need to be understood here. Firstly, Jesus 'is the same yesterday, today, and always'. Secondly, not one word of the gospel has changed. Thirdly, the church, which is made up of people like you and me, is always in need of change, of renewal. To refuse to change is to imply that we are perfect, that we have it all together, that we have fixed and firm truth. Actually, nothing could be further from the truth. The call to conversion is a call to change. With Chesterton, I believe that we never become Christians, but are always in the process of becoming. We are on a journey of change, being transformed into the image of Christ. Surely none of us could claim to have already arrived!

The process of change is like a time of gestation. This is the work of the Spirit within. It is just as when the Spirit came upon Mary, and Jesus was formed within her. There is a process of growth, of formation, of emergence. This takes time, and it requires an on-going 'yes' from me to allow it happen. Incarnation depended on Mary's 'yes'. Once that was given, the Spirit could take over, and effect the most extraordinary change and development.

Spirit and breath of God, I say 'yes' to you, so that Christ might be formed within me. Please continue the process of change, renewing my inner being, and transforming me into the image of Christ. Please bring me through the process of change that is necessary, so that I am free from everything that is not of God's making, and I am brought to the fullness of what God created me to be.

A life without change is like a stagnant pool, which is not very pretty. Jesus said that he came that we might have life, and have it to the full. The heart of a Christian is a pool into which the life of God continually flows. The heart is continually changing, and this is what we call conversion. Conversion for the soul is like breathing to the body. To stop the process of conversion is to be spiritually dead. For the Christian, this thought of constant change is exciting, and it gives rise to constant hope.

I sometimes wonder what her reaction might be if I brought my grandmother into one of the major shopping centres around town. The vast display of goods, the throngs of people, the escalators, in fact every aspect of what happens there would be beyond her ability to grasp. Bringing this one step further, I sometimes imagine myself being brought into a shopping centre a few generations from now. I cannot imagine what would confront me. The pace of change is so rapid today that it is not possible to keep track of it. I sometimes think of today's children speaking in later life about their memories of airplanes with wings, that required long runways for take-off. Who knows what memories they will have to share with their grandchildren of those days in the long distant past when everything was so much different. It is in this world that we can see the futility of someone who objects to change. The truth never changes, the gospel remains the same, and Jesus' promises still hold good. Everything else, then, can change if it will.

One of the changes that causes most problems today is the ever-growing influence of a materialistic pagan world on our values, and on our lifestyles. While I accept that this is fact, I also believe that it is relative. The world has always been changing, and it is possible that Adam and Eve had problems with some of the behaviour of their children! 'When I was your age ...!' As a Christian, I have certain values that do not change, and they will not change unless I decide otherwise. It may be more difficult to live the Christian life in today's world, but when we remember that to do so is essentially the work of the Spirit, then there is no reason to be pessimistic about it. Of myself, I do not have what it takes to live as a Christian, no matter what the world is like. Some people feel very threatened by the upheaval occurring in the church at the moment. I believe this is for the good. We had become very smug and settled in our ways. There was very little change, as if we had arrived somewhere. Vatican II was an extraordinary Pentecost. Jesus had died to bring people across a bridge from a love of law into a law of love. When I came along, the church had crossed back over that bridge into a love of law. Pope John XXIII went on his knees and asked for another Pentecost, because we had blown that first one. We got another Pentecost, and the church is coming apart and being rebuilt into a humbler, more loving church, where we will return to the teachings and mission of Jesus. This is actually a very exciting time for the church, despite the moans and groans of the doomsday prophets who would have everything remain the same, and who consider change as a harbinger of disaster. As I wrote in the chapter on Hope, the only real sin for the Christian is not to have hope. Because we are a resurrected people, we believe that Jesus has the victory, that his promises to be with the church are trustworthy and reliable, and that 'all will be well, and all manner of things will be well.'